PENGUIN BOOKS

WINNING
MATTERS

Luca,

Winning is Fun!

Kia Kaha

Sean Fitzpatrick

ALSO BY SEAN FITZPATRICK

Fronting Up: The Sean Fitzpatrick Story (with Steven O'Meagher)

Turning Point: The Making of a Captain (with Duncan Johnstone)

WINNING
MATTERS
BEING THE
BEST YOU
CAN BE

SEAN FITZPATRICK

with

ANDREW FITZGERALD

PENGUIN BOOKS

PENGUIN BOOKS
Published by the Penguin Group
Penguin Group (NZ), 67 Apollo Drive, Rosedale,
Auckland 0632, New Zealand (a division of Pearson New Zealand Ltd)
Penguin Group (USA) Inc., 375 Hudson Street,
New York, New York 10014, USA
Penguin Group (Canada), 90 Eglinton Avenue East, Suite 700, Toronto,
Ontario, M4P 2Y3, Canada (a division of Pearson Penguin Canada Inc.)
Penguin Books Ltd, 80 Strand, London, WC2R 0RL, England
Penguin Ireland, 25 St Stephen's Green,
Dublin 2, Ireland (a division of Penguin Books Ltd)
Penguin Group (Australia), 250 Camberwell Road, Camberwell,
Victoria 3124, Australia (a division of Pearson Australia Group Pty Ltd)
Penguin Books India Pvt Ltd, 11, Community Centre,
Panchsheel Park, New Delhi – 110 017, India
Penguin Books (South Africa) (Pty) Ltd, 24 Sturdee Avenue,
Rosebank, Johannesburg 2196, South Africa

Penguin Books Ltd, Registered Offices: 80 Strand, London, WC2R 0RL, England

First published by Penguin Group (NZ), 2011

Designed and typeset by Anna Egan-Reid, © Penguin Group (NZ)
Printed and bound in Australia by Griffin Press

ISBN 9780143565901

A catalogue record for this book is available
from the National Library of New Zealand.

www.penguin.co.nz

CONTENTS

FOREWORD

AFTER THE MATCH, ENGLAND'S INTERNATIONAL rugby stadium in Twickenham emptied 40,000 fans out of its stands; music blaring, and raucous crowds clamouring for another beer and a sing-song. It was an international game, but not involving England. Instead, Twickenham was hosting the All Blacks, New Zealand's fearsome rugby team, against the Barbarians in their last match of a tour before heading home. It was an invitation fifteen made up of established international players, the occasional superstar and a sprinkling of up-and-coming talent from around the rugby world. The match had been all about one man, Bryan Habana. Young, gifted and black, Habana played for the South African team, the Springboks, as their pace man, their high-speed, jinking, accelerating phenomenon who had officially run faster than a cheetah in a publicity stunt the previous year. This afternoon he had pulled on the Barbarian jersey, scored three tries and played an integral part in a great match that ended with the Barbarians memorably beating the All Blacks.

Around the stadium are the hospitality boxes, where the great and the good congregate. In one of them, Sean Fitzpatrick was chewing the fat with a couple of other ex-internationals – one English player and a South African. Outside, two 10-year-old lads caught his eye and waved to him. He excused himself from his illustrious company, came outside, shook each of their hands, said hello and asked them how they enjoyed the game. He listened intently, nodding and smiling, agreeing and questioning, and before long the three of them were engrossed in a post-match analysis.

I happened to be watching because one of them was my son, Archie. Sean didn't know either Archie or his mate Mattie, and although he knew me because we had worked together on a business project, he hadn't made any connection between the two young lads and me. To him, they were just a couple of kids waving at him, and the fact that he took the time and had the courtesy to meet the lads and spend a few minutes with them speaks volumes about the bloke. Of course, I then came out of the shadows and broke the spell by demanding a beer. Seano hoisted us over the barrier and into the box where the boys had a fantastic hour supping free fizzy drink and looking at the international jerseys on the wall, while Sean told them all about the teams and the players to whom they belonged. Magical.

There is indeed something magical about the game of rugby. I've been a fan for as long as I can remember (I played from eight until my late thirties and now I coach my lad's team) and right from my very earliest rugby memories, the All Blacks loomed large – a brilliant, untouchable, romantic team. And I distinctly remember watching

S.B.T. Fitzpatrick play. His aggressive, uncompromising approach was brutally compelling. He was a one-man wrecking machine in the loose, a great scrummager, always on the money with his line-out throwing, and he got around the park too. He had it all, he brought a whole new dimension to the position of hooker and he set the standard that remains to this day the benchmark of excellence. And aside from being the best Number 2 in the world, he was also an inspirational leader. Between 1986 and 1997 he played 128 matches for the All Blacks. Of those, 92 were Test matches, and a record 51 of those were as captain.

Some months after our meeting at Twickenham, I had the distinct pleasure of walking to the Millennium Stadium in Cardiff alongside Sean when the All Blacks were in town, taking on France in the Rugby World Cup. On his way to do the TV commentary, he was looking sharp in his New Zealand blazer, pressed trousers, black polished shoes, and All Black tie, perfectly knotted. We walked through the busy centre of Cardiff and there was a fantastic atmosphere. Rugby fans were everywhere, spilling out of the bars and pubs, having a few drinks in the afternoon sun, singing and waving flags in anticipation of the game.

Every few yards of that 20-minute walk, Sean was recognised. Big burly Kiwis nodded to him respectfully; people stopped him and shook his hand; fans waved and shouted 'All right Fitzy' or started chanting his name; we were waylaid half a dozen times for pictures to be taken. And Sean was relaxed, comfortable, and happy. He chatted away to whoever approached him. I was pretty much invisible, but Sean? He was clearly a hero among his people.

Just after Sean retired, Kevin Roberts of Saatchi and Saatchi wrote the foreword for Sean's autobiography, in which he said, 'I believe Sean will be successful in whatever field he chooses and he's built for long-term success. He's a self-made man, he's not flash, he has these very human qualities – there's a little bit of Sean in all of us. Yet he also has those very strong values of success, leadership, loyalty, integrity – all these good things that you don't see too much of these days.' That just about sums Sean up, and Kevin continued by suggesting that, 'A future book will, I hope, tell the story of Sean's further metamorphosis from All Black legend to successful entrepreneur, once again stretching the boundaries of his potential.' Prescient indeed . . . not just because of the work that Sean now does, but because it does absolutely nail the fact that Sean pushes himself, stretches boundaries, and takes things on.

What is clear from getting to know Sean's story is that good fortune has played its part in his career. He was consistently in the right place at the right time – to get his first cap, to play in the Rugby World Cup, and ultimately to be chosen as the captain of the All Blacks. But for me, what has been even more striking, even more evident, is the fact that whenever an opportunity has presented itself, he has been ready, willing and able to step up and deliver. Sean has always worked hard to put himself in the position of being able to make opportunity count . . . and once he gets hold of something, he never lets it go. A romantic would perhaps have come off the pitch just before the end of the World Cup Final in 1987 to allow Andy Dalton, the more senior (and original pre-tournament choice for Sean's position) to come on, even if just for the last couple of minutes. Sean? No way. It was his position now, and he intended to keep it that way. To my mind, that is a key factor in his success.

In suggesting that we put this book together, Sean did so humbly. Not one ounce of it was about the big 'I am'. It was – is – about saying,

'Look, here are some of the things I've done and some of the things I think I've learnt along the way. Take a look, and if you think they might be of use to you, then it has been a worthwhile exercise.' I know that if Sean gets a single person thanking him for the book because it pointed them in the right direction, or gave them a clue about what to do in their own life, he will be delighted.

For my part, simply to have the opportunity to spend huge chunks of time talking about rugby with an all-time great who also happens to be a really good bloke has been a real privilege. I have thoroughly and hugely enjoyed putting this book together with Sean. Like him, I hope that you enjoy it.

Andy FitzGerald

INTRODUCTION

IT WAS LATE AT NIGHT, the heater was humming and Mum and Dad were absently listening to the radio as we drove home. I can't remember where we'd been exactly – I must have only been seven or eight at the time – but the four of us Fitzpatrick kids were half-dozing on the bench seat in the back. I recall as clearly as if it were yesterday my father suddenly stepping on the brakes and then backing up, just as we drove through a quiet intersection in town. Dad got out of the car and thunked the door closed. He strode across the dark, silent street and we watched him go, with no idea what was going on until we saw, on the other side of the road, a man lying prone and unmoving in the gutter. I was the youngest and I was absolutely petrified; I thought the man was dead, or worse, an escaped madman who was about to jump up and kill us all. The terror that gripped me for those few seconds remains with me to this day.

Of course he was neither as it turned out. He was just a bloke who had taken a bit too much beer on board, was the worse for wear and in need of a lie down . . . we've all been there! Dad woke him up, got him back on his feet again, and after chatting amiably to him for a minute or two, waved him on his way home.

It may only seem like an insignificant incident; certainly my dad made no song and dance about it. He just got back into the car, said a couple of words of explanation to Mum, then released the handbrake and off we went. I am sure he didn't give it another thought, but I think it says a good deal about him. It is a specific moment from my childhood when I remember having a huge amount of admiration for Dad – not just his bravery in tackling a potential murderer, but in his straightforward reaction. No fuss, no fanfare, just a good man helping another bloke out. It was perhaps the first time that I became conscious of, or thought consciously about, the values that my dad possessed. I saw him in that moment as a strong, solid man with a big heart. That incident has stuck with me to this day.

Years and years later, I was sitting in my car on Queen Street, the main area for shopping in central Auckland, waiting outside a shop while Bronnie, my wife, was running in to get something. A fight broke out across the road. There were two cops getting into a spot of bother with some young hooligans, so I nipped over and gave them a hand. I got a lovely letter from the police afterwards and I was inordinately proud of myself – not because I was an upstanding citizen or anything, but because I have absolutely no doubt that Dad would have done exactly the same thing, and the thought that some of him had rubbed off on me made me very happy. I was proud of

There are common threads that hold true whether you are running in tries, running for office, or running a family or a business.

the fact that my dad had, through his actions all those years before, taught me a lesson.

In my formative years as a rugby player at school, I had the great fortune to be coached by a fellow called Guy Davis. The team I played in wasn't a great outfit; we all knew that – in fact, we were probably the worst rugby team at school, but Guy's world-view was fantastic, and he was also to teach me a lesson and an approach that has stayed with me through my playing days and remains at the heart of the values that I hold dear today. It was a simple and straightforward message that everybody in the team understood. He told us over and over again that it didn't matter what level of talent had been given to us, what size we were or how fast or slow we ran. It was what we *did* with the talent that we had that counted. We were expected to strive to be as successful as we could be with whatever we had been given, no excuses and no exceptions. 'The only thing I want you to be,' he explained, 'is the best that you can possibly be.'

Be the best you can be.

That simple notion resonated so clearly and loudly that I have carried it with me ever since, and it is a perfect example of an important life lesson that I have learnt from the game of rugby. But what follows isn't *just* a rugby book. Or at least I hope it isn't. The way things have turned out, I've led a very privileged and exciting life, and that has been due to the game of rugby – so of course the sport has to figure in here. However, I wanted to write more than just a series of reminiscences or anecdotes that would mean I'd probably only end up repeating stories I've already written about in my earlier autobiography *Fronting Up*. Instead I wanted to write about the wider game of life as well.

Of course, almost anything I do write is inevitably tinged with rugby. It has been a massive part of my life. As a player I had the good fortune to play for the greatest rugby team on the planet – the New Zealand All Blacks. For Kiwis, the All Black team – a national side steeped in over a century's history and laden with tradition and stories and myth – represents and encapsulates New Zealand culture. There is a fierce expectation both at home and around the world that, whatever the competition, wherever the game is played, and whoever the game is played against, the All Blacks will win. The All Black team is both a cornerstone and a touchstone of New Zealand culture. The nation supports the team, and the team gives identity to the nation. It gives us Kiwis a worldwide legitimacy, and we believe that it not only represents and stands for all that is good about New Zealand, but it is also what sets us apart. Throughout my international playing career of eleven years, I was involved in some wonderful times: playing in and winning the inaugural Rugby World Cup in 1987, for example – heady times. Some years later in 1996, I also had the privilege of being the captain that led the first ever All Black side to a series victory against South Africa on their home soil. Back then, the Springboks were – and in fact they remain – our biggest rugby rival and oldest foe. They are a side for whom we have a healthy respect. So beating them in their own backyard repeatedly was fantastic . . . ahh, the list of good times goes on. But, before I really *do* turn this Introduction into a potted autobiography, I should move on. What I am trying to say is that I have been one lucky man and I am immensely grateful to the game for giving me so many fond and deeply held memories.

Happily for me it didn't all end with my last match against Wales in 1997. Hanging up my boots turned out to be the start of another adventure: moving into business, and carving out a new life on the

It didn't matter what level of talent had been given to us, what size we were or how fast or slow we ran. It was what we did with the talent that we had that counted.

other side of the world. After my career ended, coming to England made good sense to me. It was a great opportunity for me to build something up for myself and my family on the other side of the world; it was an adventure. Still is. And things haven't slowed down at all. I'm pleased to say that I'm busier than ever with a wide range of different projects which I was recently told is a 'portfolio career'. Sounds rather grand, but in fact it is just me making the most of my time, and trying to keep busy! With my wife, Bronwyn, I run a corporate hospitality business; I do speaking engagements on a pretty regular basis; I have a consultancy company, of which I am very proud, and which looks to take the lessons from international rugby and leadership into businesses. I also do some TV work, and a reasonable amount of column writing for newspapers. I'm still a huge rugby fan, and I sit on the board of Harlequins Rugby Club in London. It's a good life.

Of course, every once in a while I still get a twinge of nostalgia, remembering what it was like to be right there in the middle of it all. I have such fond memories of pulling the black jersey on, but I know that part of my life is over now. Time marches inevitably on, and mostly I cope with it. I am hugely grateful for the opportunity to live the life I have now, and it is all down to rugby. The game has certainly opened all manner of doors and opportunities to me. I have met some great folk, and I think I have learnt some important things about people and about myself along the way.

So this book is about those two things. First of all, it is about some of the interesting people I've met before, during and after my time as an All Black, and not just the rugby players, but lots of different people who in some way – in their own way – have made this a fascinating journey. Secondly though, and perhaps more importantly, it is about what I've *learnt* from the people I have met along the way. Having been lucky enough to scrum down (literally and metaphorically) with so many different people, in putting this book together I have been reflecting on what I've learnt from them. It has become increasingly clear to me that there have been a number of significant moments and meetings in my life where I have changed or developed in how I look at the world. Different people and experiences have taught me (and continue to teach me) invaluable lessons about what is important, and about how to act, react and behave. I firmly believe that my 'world-view' (meaning how I see the world, not my view on how to fix it!) is the sum of all these experiences. Some have taught me by example, by the way they have acted. Others have reinforced values and beliefs which I hold dear. A few, by what they have (or have not) done, have provided me with negative examples and been powerful contra-indicators of what to do or how to behave. The point is that wherever and however these lessons have presented themselves, what seems to have emerged for me is a set of very consistent and cohesive principles that I hold as both important and valuable to me.

I do believe that there are common threads that hold true whether you are running in tries, running for office or running a family or a business. It seems to me that there are similarities and commonalities in people who are good at what they do; that the lines between sport and business and life are blurred; that there are common threads of excellence that universally hold true. They are important threads too – because woven together they represent the fabric of your life and it is these that guide you through the challenges and opportunities that come your way.

What I have done in this book is try to break down and lay out these threads, these beliefs and principles, in the hope that they will be of some value and interest to you, and in the hope that by so doing

I remember having a huge amount of admiration for Dad . . . no fuss, no fanfare, just a good man helping another bloke out.

I can perhaps provide you with specific ideas that, when applied to your own situations and challenges, will be of help to you. I certainly don't want you to think that I am suggesting that I can provide all the answers to the myriad of problems that come our way, or that I have necessarily unlocked any of life's great secrets, but what I do know is that these beliefs and principles have served me well, and that I have turned to them again and again as I have gone through my life so far. So I have set them down here, to at least provide you with some ideas and thoughts that might be useful to you. I believe that they form a basis upon which you can build your own solutions and directions. By providing you with specific tools and actions, I hope that I will have been able to give you something to build on, to strengthen and develop for yourself and your own use. For anyone looking to find shape and direction in what they do or how they do it, or looking to do something different to move matters along, I hope that some of the lessons I have learnt will prove to be a useful springboard.

So, whoever you are, wherever you are, and whatever you do, I sincerely hope that within this book you will find ideas that will help you to do things differently, or to try something new. Becoming the best you can be is a continuous, never-ending process, and, in my most optimistic moments, I would like to think that some of the things I write about will give people an insight; that this book might say something specific that will be helpful, that will spark a thought, or give someone a different way to approach a problem or an opportunity that they face. I hope so.

Enjoy the book.

Oh and, of course, 'Go the All Blacks!'

Sean

ONE

BE THE BEST YOU CAN BE

THE NEW ZEALAND THAT MY father was born into was a very different place to that of today – it really was another world. Decades before the internet and cheap flights brought it into the wider global consciousness, it was a remote island nation, just beyond the middle of nowhere, and more or less on the other side of the world, no matter where you happened to be from. It was a tough existence for many, and it bred tough people and tough communities – fiercely self-sufficient, hard-working, but (with many families rooted in Celtic culture) a people well able to let their hair down when the occasion or need arose.

Dad's mother died when he was very young, and as his father was an Irish-born forestry worker who was often out working for days on end in the bush. My dad went to live in Gisborne with his aunt and uncle, Chris and Tom Corkery. Gisborne is situated in the North East of the country, located at the northern end of Poverty Bay and, interestingly and to my mind somewhat romantically, the first city in the world to greet the sun each day. His aunt and uncle lived right on the beach and by the sounds of it, even with money being tight, Dad led quite the life. He was one of those young superstars who was great at pretty much any sport he turned his hand to. He surfed (why wouldn't he with the beach at his door?!), was a great competitive swimmer and as he grew up he became head of the lifesaving club. He ran everywhere. I remember him saying, 'Son, when I left school and started at the bank, I used to run five miles to work and five miles back again at the end of the day.' He used to race the cars between the power poles too – so it wasn't just running, it was sprinting in phases as well; basically a fantastic training session every day, topped off with a swim and a surf at the end, no doubt. No wonder that, even years later, he had such a bloody good engine on him!

At school my dad played rugby for the 1st XV (the best school team) for three consecutive years – quite a feat – and he captained the side too. When he left school to work in the bank in Gisborne, he continued playing the game that is ingrained into Kiwi culture. He became an All Black out of Poverty Bay when he was a young man; in fact he was only 19 years old at the time. He toured to Australia in 1950–51 where he picked up a knee injury and then, after recovering, he moved to Wellington to play for Victoria University and was later selected for the 1953–54 tour to Britain (where the All Blacks beat England, Scotland and Ireland, but lost to Wales). After that tour Dad didn't play for them again. At that stage he was 22 or 23, and to have achieved so much at such a young age is a clear indication of the type of man he was. Playing a game that everybody played, Dad had become one of the country's very best. At a very young age he had achieved at the very highest level. He had pulled on the black jersey of the All Blacks.

BACKGROUND: HISTORY OF THE ALL BLACKS

Rugby Football was first introduced to New Zealand by a Mr Charles Monro in the late 1860s, after he had played it while studying in England. The sport quickly took hold in the country, spreading from town to town and region to region, and, on 15 August 1903, at the Sydney Cricket Ground, the New Zealand rugby team's first true international test match against Australia took place. It was a 22–3 win; a good start and a sign of things to come.

The first touring New Zealand squad, referred to as The Originals, toured Britain two years later in 1905 and it was here that the All Black name became associated with the team. One of the more colourful theories as to the origins of the name suggests that a London newspaper, reporting on one of their first games, described the style of play as one where the New Zealanders played as if they were 'all backs' (a rugby team is divided into bigger, slower forwards, and smaller, lighter, more mobile and speedy backs). Legend has it that then, because of a typographical error, subsequent references were made to the 'All Blacks'. You can believe that if you like, and it is certainly a romantic notion, but I've always maintained the key factor was the fact that when they played, their jerseys, shorts and socks were indeed all black! You decide . . . but, either way, it was great branding, and The Originals tourists won every match bar one (and that was a heavily disputed match against the Welsh that we Kiwis are still convinced we won!). In their ferocity, innovation and grace, they laid the foundations of what has since proved to be an imperious rugby dynasty spanning more than a century. Over subsequent decades, the lure of the All Blacks grew and grew, and their repeated ability to win added to the fascination. They became the international rugby team that everybody wanted to see, and the team that everyone wanted to beat. The All Blacks became the yardstick by which any nation would measure themselves . . . although statistically few do measure up; the All Blacks overall win percentage, in over 100 years of tough international and touring rugby, is a staggering 75 per cent, and they have a winning record against every international side they have played, including South Africa and the British and Irish Lions.

This rugby team has come to represent New Zealand so deeply and completely that every Kiwi is part-All Black; everybody has a stake in the team that epitomises everything that we stand for, that we are proud of – our spirit and our cultural heritage, our fight and our desire. All Blacks have a fierce loyalty to the jersey and each other. They work bloody hard. They have a deep sense of history and tradition. They are tough and uncompromising. They play the game the way it should be played. And they win.

The combination of all these things makes the All Blacks a team to watch wherever you are in the world, but it becomes even more potent and powerful because on top of all that, for most people, the All Blacks come from a tiny island nation on the other side of the world; I am sure that this distance has made the story and the journey more romantic and compelling.

There is an aura, an intangible difference which separates the All Blacks from every other international rugby team that is more than just the sum of all the parts. Formula One has Ferrari, football has Brazil, rugby has the All Blacks.

Dad enjoyed life too. He was a highly sociable bloke who knew how to have a good time. He enjoyed a drink, and was always in the middle of things. Mum met him at a twenty-first birthday party in Auckland, a first meeting that was, if not romantic, then certainly memorable. As Mum arrived at this house party where the parents were absent (always a bad idea), she walked through to the lounge and was confronted by some tall, handsome fella, clearly a rugby player, with a beer in one hand and a push-powered lawn-mower in the other. He was walking up and down in beautifully straight lines, mowing the shag pile carpet. That picture still makes me laugh – because it was such a lovely first meeting, but also at the thought of the returning home-owner looking at his carpet quizzically, reasonably convinced but not entirely certain, that his shag had been a little more 'piley' the week before . . .

Whether it is preparing your boots, playing for the All Blacks, working in a shop, or being a father or a bus conductor, you can decide to take an approach that doesn't allow compromise.

Dad carried on playing rugby a little while longer after he retired from the All Blacks; he even beat the Springboks in 1956 with the New Zealand Universities side – one of his fondest rugby memories – and then ran out for Auckland for a while, but by 1960 he was all done on the playing front. While he never lost any of his competitive edge and remained an excellent squash player for many years to come, by 1961 he had retired from the rugby pitch and settled into family life. I was born a few years later in 1963 – the youngest of four children.

So, because my dad had finished his rugby by the time I came along, his All Black career always seemed remote, miles away from us as kids growing up. He wasn't one for wearing his achievements loudly, and there was very little in the way of rugby memorabilia round the house. It was a well-used, busy family home, so maybe there just wasn't any space for a shrine to past glories; Dad would never have wanted anything like that – it was just way too flashy for him.

I recall one day when my brother and I were playing around in the garage. Like most people's garages, it was full to brimming with stuff: musty over-stacked cupboards, step ladders and golf clubs, oil cans, tools and benches, bikes and jumble – for us boys it was an Aladdin's cave, a treasure trove. We clambered under and round and over, hunting, rooting through boxes and looking on the highest shelves for hidden deadly acid and rummaging in tool-kits for any hitherto undiscovered ray-gun weaponry. Then Mark opened up a dusty old box sitting in a corner. It was full of old rugby jerseys. We pulled them out one by one; big, heavy jerseys, beautifully thick, with intricately embroidered badges. The jerseys were those that Dad had collected throughout his international career, swapped with opponents at the end of games from all over the world. They were absolutely fascinating, spellbinding, to Mark and me. They told of exotic locations and distant battles . . . and most of all they were *All Black* related. We had no idea Dad had them, and in the absence of much else around the house, it was solid tangible evidence, right there in our hands, of his stature and pedigree within the game. When Dad came out to the garage and saw us looking at them, he was very matter of fact as he put them back in their box; in fact, I think he didn't really like talking about his playing days to us, in case it might have been seen as blowing his own trumpet.

Of course, I never saw him play. I suppose in a way I have regrets about that, but perhaps the distance between his career and my own life was a blessing – certainly I never felt pressured by having an All Black father. By not having that shadow of paternal excellence and achievement visibly hanging over me, I was allowed to develop at my own pace and not be pressurised by expectation. The separation that existed between Dad's international career and us kids paid dividends as we grew up, no doubt; and the humility he showed was an important part of who Dad was and how he lived his life.

Dad was big on *values* – he used, and lived by, words like 'honesty', 'respect' and 'integrity'. He drilled us in our pleases and thank-you's. He was caring, open and gregarious, wonderful with friends, and the house was always full of people. I remember him often, up early, busy and happy and humming, cooking a full breakfast for all the people that were staying over in the beach house – he loved all that.

And he was a bit of a hard bastard, too. He would smack us. Mum would give us fair warning. She'd say to Mark and me when we'd been naughty (and we *were* naughty!), 'When your dad gets home you are going to get a smack!' And when he came back, the court would sit. Counsel would be short and sweet; guilty as charged. And then we'd lie over his knee and he'd bloody whack us! Right on the arse. I suppose these days it would be seen as terrible child abuse, but the thing I can remember most about those episodes is that while I was getting whacked, Mark – somewhere out of Dad's eyeline – would be standing there grinning or pulling faces. And while he was getting his turn, I would try to do the same. And it was the funniest thing in the world. Perhaps a little bizarrely, they're happy memories! I recall too how sometimes the four of us kids would be in the back of the car and we'd be fighting and annoying each other and generally being rowdy and boisterous. Dad would simply put his belt on the dashboard and tell us in no uncertain terms that he didn't want to hear another word out of any of us. Of course, a few seconds later – in absolute silence – we'd be prodding and poking and pinching each other, trying to get the other person to squeak or cry or laugh so they'd get a whack. And as the youngest, you can guess who probably got the short end of the stick most often!

In fact I do recall spending a lot of my younger life fighting: fighting to keep up with the older ones; fighting for my own space and identity; to have my voice heard; and every once in a while fighting physically, almost for my life (or so it felt!), when my sisters and brother decided to let me know who was boss! It was a natural pecking order, and I think it made me strong and feisty. But I was still a scaredy cat . . .

We lived two miles from a cemetery and to get back to our house from town, you could turn right at a particular junction and take a short-cut through the graveyard. I would be frightened; going through the cemetery with all its ghosts and buried dead bodies just plain terrified us kids. Particularly if we were driving home in the car at night, we would all be pleading with Dad, 'Please don't go through the cemetery,' and I am sure I would be screaming the loudest. He would say, 'Yeah, yeah, it'll be all right, don't worry', and drive through the cemetery anyway. His shoulders would be shaking with laughter, and we'd hear him chuckling to himself as we drove through. I think he probably knew it was a bit naughty, but thought that it was just plain funny. Which it was. I look back on that now and it still makes me smile.

To this day, though, when I hear a noise downstairs or a bump in the night, I always wake my wife and say to her, 'You go and see what it is Bronnie!' while I stay in bed with the duvet over my head. All these years later and I still get that 'driving through the cemetery' feeling!

Friday nights were the big nights in our house: fish and chips for tea and then sitting in front of the TV with Dad and Mark. We had one of those old shoemaker's irons, and we used to put the boots on it one by one, pulling the sprigs (studs) out, whacking the nails in, and generally cleaning them and prepping them for the weekend's rugby. Dad always used to say, 'Always have clean boots, son', 'Always have your socks up, son', 'Tidy, neat and nippy, son, that's what you need to be.' Good advice. Those Friday night rituals taught me the importance of preparation. Come Saturday's game I was always the same: clean boots, socks up, ready to play. While there might be a million things that you can't control – the size of the opposition or the way the referee interprets the laws, for example – you absolutely can choose to control those things that you do have influence over, and to do so to the very best of your ability. Whether it is preparing your boots, playing for the All Blacks, working in a shop, or being a father or a bus conductor, you can decide to take an approach that doesn't allow compromise. Whatever it is, you can set out to be the very best you can be. That single idea has in many ways become the mantra for my life. Incredibly simple, but potentially immensely

Dad was big on *values* – he used, and lived by, words like 'honesty', 'respect' and 'integrity'. He drilled us in our pleases and thank-you's. He was caring, open and gregarious, wonderful with friends, and the house was always full of people.

powerful. 'Become the best you can be' is a notion that I came across first through how my dad behaved, and then in how my school coach, Guy Davis, talked to me, and it has been my compass and map on the road I've taken since. I have made it central to how I think about my life and how I continually strive to approach it. It is certainly an approach that you recognise in others when you see it. When you meet a person who is striving to be the best they can be, you notice. When you set out to become the best you can be, the very act of deciding is a powerful moment.

AN IDEA TO TRY: BECOMING THE BEST YOU CAN BE

If you are going to be at your best, you need to have a think about when and why that is. You need to be clear about where the lines are in your life that you won't cross, and you need to have a view on where you're going to. So take a look at the following three questions. They're deceptively difficult – the sorts of questions that the more you think about them, the harder (and more revealing) they become, so take some time to work through your answer.

When are you at your best?

What are you really good at?

What is your ultimate goal?

Knowing your own answers to these questions is powerful. To be able to honestly appraise yourself is a valuable asset. Aim to have a short paragraph written down for each of these questions – the third one in particular. What is your ultimate goal? Write your answer down. To have your ideal end-point written down – and kept in a place where you can see it, re-read it, become familiar with it – makes it more real and gives it shape. If you don't put it down on paper, it remains a thought. When it is there in black and white, it becomes something more solid. It gives you something to aim at. Write it down. Read it. Aim for it.

As a perfect example of this idea, a man came around to the house the other week – a local guy from Windsor, a pest control specialist. Bronnie and I thought we might have wasps in our attic, and so we called this guy out of the phone book, he came out to have a look and disappeared up into the loft space. It turns out that we did have a nest, so off he went to get his kit out of the van. Now let me tell you, that pest control specialist was the perfect demonstration of the 'be the best you can be' principle in action. He absolutely enthused about his work. He wanted to do his job quickly and professionally, and we could see that it was important to him. As he worked, he told us all about the different types of wasps and nests, and about how they build them. He had facts, figures and stories tumbling out of him. He was quick, neat, organised and by the time he left, Bronnie, myself and the kids were almost experts! A great guy.

Another example is a football manager called Aidy Boothroyd. When he was the manager of Watford Town FC, he asked me to pop up there and meet with the team. I was delighted to accept Aidy's invitation, and was keen to have a nosey round a Premiership club –

It doesn't matter if you are president of a global corporation, the guy who comes round to remove the wasps' nest from the roof space, or the rookie new boy in a team of big tough bastards who scare the pants off you . . . being the best you can be is about doing what you do, and doing it as well as you can.

which at that stage they were, although they were struggling with the intensity and demands as a newly promoted club and looked destined to drop back down again that same season.

Driving up there, I wondered about the differences and similarities I could expect to see compared with a rugby team. First of all, the age of the guys surprised me; they were a young crew of lads and for many of them I guess it was a tough place to be (at the bottom of the league and struggling in a small club) so early on in their footy careers. The second noticeable fact of course was the size. There were no big muscle-bound locks gnawing on the benches, these lads were real athletes – we played very different games, of course, but their physiology was strikingly different.

But for all those differences, the reason Aidy Boothroyd asked me to come in was because he was trying to impart the same message to his lads – be the best you can possibly be. Football and rugby are about results. Aidy was running a good, tight club with comparatively limited resources, and he was clear that nurturing and maintaining a winning mentality was going to be vital in the coming weeks and months. Even given a lack of resources and a small squad, he wanted to ensure that his team was the best it could possibly be. I liked that approach.

But it is a hard work option. There's no substitute for hard work. Of all the basic rules that underpin success, I guess this is the most quoted. Well, I am someone who absolutely subscribes to that view, and being the best you can be more often than not means putting your shoulder down and bloody grafting for it. I can remember spending hours out on the pitch after training had officially finished, practising my line-out throws, sometimes blindfolding myself to make it a little bit tougher. Of course, there have been mercurial talents that managed to float through life without hard work, but the truly exceptional, the absolutely outstanding athletes and business people in this world get up, get going and work at it, hard, all the time, relentlessly.

I think that as a player I did that, but that certainly doesn't give me the right to sit back on my laurels and relax now that I'm retired. If anything, in fact, the opposite is true. I still have to be the best I can be in whatever I turn my hand to. International rugby may be a little bit beyond me now but in its place there is journalism, commentating, after-dinner speaking, charity work, business coaching; and all of it I have to do to the best of my ability. But I do have to keep working at it. Every once in a while I sit back and think that maybe I should be looking at doing more. I need to keep going back to that principle and checking myself against it. It is a simple test I apply to myself on a pretty regular basis. It is very easy to get comfortable or complacent and before you know it days turn into weeks turn into years and you're left behind, out of date, and you've lost your focus. We all need to keep learning and keep improving and changing, or else we get left behind. Charles Darwin said that the species that will be the most successful is the one that can manage change most successfully. It isn't just about being fast, or strong, it is about being able to apply whatever talents you've got in the best way possible. You have to adapt to the changing situation and continually ask yourself how you can do things better.

AN IDEA TO TRY: HOW CAN I . . . ?

Being the best you can be is a broad title. Break it down a little bit, into smaller chunks that you can more easily manage. Be more specific. In what areas of your life do you want to be the best you can be?

Make this a two-part exercise for yourself. First of all, write down the areas in which you would like to be the best you can be. When you've done that, spend time looking at each one and consider the 'how'? How are you going to achieve that? Keep coming back to this word 'how', because it moves your thought process from 'can I?' to 'how can I?'. It unlocks and unblocks and it starts to focus on action, on doing something positive.

How do you work out how to be the best? Well, first of all you have to define what the 'best' is. Take a look around you. Read, watch, listen, absorb, analyse. Take inspiration and direction from wherever you can find it, but spend some time sitting down and working through what 'best' actually means for you in your chosen field. When you've done that, it is simply a matter of breaking the end-point down into achievable next steps.

The critical ingredient, though, is that you have the inspiration in the first place, so seek it out, look to *be* inspired. Whether you have to map it out on a sheet of paper and put a written plan together, or whether you just know what is required next and you are crystal clear, it doesn't matter. There is an old adage that says, 'If you don't know where you're going, any road will take you there.' There is real value in stopping, thinking, and working out where you are, what being the best means for you, and then what you need to do to get there. If it sounds a little simplistic, I make no apologies. Woody Allen said something like '90 per cent of success is just turning up', and he was spot on. By getting focused and starting to work towards specific goals and targets, you're already well on the way to being the best that you can be.

AN IDEA TO TRY: SHARE YOUR GOALS

Articulate your dream. Share it. Tell people. Commit to your dreams by letting people know. People will want to help, encourage and see you making progress towards it. Of course there may be those who are disparaging or unsupportive, but that speaks more about their unhappy map of the world than about you. Nevertheless, share your goals and aspirations – it is a good thing, it energises you and the process of talking about it gives you motivation – if for no other reason than fear of failure after telling people! Be prepared to tell people how you're going to get there too – they're bound to ask. A sure-fire way to keep a dream on the 'sometime but not now' list is to keep it quiet. So be brave – tell someone.

There's no substitute for hard work . . . being the best you can be more often than not means putting your shoulder down and bloody grafting for it.

Hanging my boots up was a time when I had to apply this thinking to my own situation. I was concerned about what the future held. I certainly didn't want to be one of those ex-players who walked backwards into the future, just spending his life at rugby dinners re-telling tales and living off the glories of yesterday (although they do pay well and I'm certainly up for a free meal, a beer and a yarn every once in a while!). Bronnie, myself, and my good friend Kevin Roberts (who you'll meet a couple of times in this book) talked at great length about my targets and goals after finishing playing. I set myself specific goals and targets to pursue, and although they have changed and developed over time, that process was invaluable to me in focusing on the future rather than the past. And as part of those goals and targets, I have ensured that I have maintained a healthy exercise regime and lifestyle. I still make sure I find time to push myself occasionally, either playing golf, or sculling up and down the Thames – a sport that I thoroughly enjoy. When I play golf or when I row, I set myself targets and goals; and not always easy ones either. I say to myself, *Seano, if you want to win today you're going to have to up your game!* I think that is really important. Challenging yourself. Because if you don't challenge yourself, you'll end up settling for second best, and that *is* a crime.

AN IDEA TO TRY: BE THE BEST YOU CAN BE TODAY!

Why not have five things that you can do this week that will challenge you in some way? Not a turgid, must-tidy-my-desk job list, but a list of small specific actions or goals that will push you a bit further than you've been pushed today (or before). Even the tiniest step forward takes you closer to being the best you can be, so train yourself to demand a little bit more from yourself than you did yesterday. Challenge yourself, teach yourself to compete. You take 11 minutes to walk to the bus stop? Do it in 10. It will put your heart rate up a little bit, stretch the legs a bit more. Setting challenges and goals that you can carry with you during the day hones the competitive side of your nature. The process of aiming to do something faster/quicker/slower/more completely/more accurately means you are developing a way of thinking where the setting and achieving of goals becomes second nature. It shows you that you can be better. You can improve.

A FINAL THOUGHT ON BEING THE BEST YOU CAN BE

There is genuine enjoyment in striving to become the best you can be, whatever you do. The wasp man and I share that. Because it doesn't matter if you are president of a global corporation, the guy who comes round to remove the wasps' nest from the roof space, or the rookie new boy in a team of big tough bastards who scare the pants off you . . . being the best you can be is about doing what you do, and doing it as well as you can. It means developing and maintaining enthusiasm for whatever it is you do, having belief in the value and importance of hard work, and harbouring a desire to do your thing – whatever that is – as well as you possibly can.

When you see people working to become the very best they can be, it is infectious, attractive and compelling. Being the best you can be is bloody difficult . . . but very rewarding. It is a direction in life that will mean you demand more of yourself, and then more again, but it is absolutely worth it.

TWO

GETTING WHAT YOU WANT

SO WHAT DID I WANT to be when I was growing up? To be honest I am not entirely sure. I don't recall any intense burning ambition that stayed with me all the way through childhood. I can certainly remember that part of me at some stage wanted to be a fireman, although I suspect that was probably only because as a kid I used to get my hair cut next to the fire station. I don't think at that time in my life I really knew what I wanted, I was just happy doing my thing. And I hadn't got any serious notion or expectation of becoming an All Black either. Of course, I'd play games with my brother where we'd re-enact international matches, but because I was the youngest I always ended up as South Africa or England or sometimes, even worse, Australia . . . and always ended up losing too, just like in real life!

I did dream about playing for the All Blacks, but I'm not so sure it was necessarily any different, any more well-formed, than the dreams of many a young soccer fan pulling on his favourite club's football shirt and imagining that he's scoring the winner at Wembley, when in fact he's bouncing a cheap plastic ball off the side of a shed in his backyard; or a kid standing on his own on a windy pitch with a rugby ball, eyeing up the posts with grim determination and about to kick a penalty, imagining a whole nation holding its breath as he does so. And of course I had heroes that I wanted to be like, in the same way that Richie McCaw, or Dan Carter are held up as heroes now by a whole generation of kids.

My hero in those days was Bryan Williams. What a guy. He exploded onto the scene as the All Black winger of Polynesian descent who had pace, power and a prodigious sidestep, which is a hard skill to really master (and some of us never did!). He played well over one hundred times for the All Blacks, and remains to this day one of the best players ever in that position. His sidestep was indeed legendary. Here was a guy who could run like the wind, and then, in full stride and at top velocity, step fully two metres to the side without appearing to slow down. I distinctly remember Mark, myself and some friends marking out the two-metre sidestep on the pitch, and then accelerating up to top speed and trying to do the same thing. Of course we failed – it was almost inconceivable that a man could do it at all. Bryan Williams could though. He was an All Black god, and I for one worshipped him. I still wonder today if maybe this was the first time that I developed an aspiration in terms of what I wanted to be. Albeit subconsciously, by wanting to be like Williams, I was perhaps setting my sights for the first time on becoming an All Black.

There are two types of players in a rugby team, piano movers and piano players. It was clear that my body shape meant I was never going to be one of the piano players, so I put down the music and lowered my shoulder.

Back at home, Mum used to wash the club jerseys for Mark's team every week – and from my very earliest memories I can remember playing in the garden and seeing these 15 jerseys hung out on the line to dry, flapping around, numbers upside down, huge.

Growing up in New Zealand in the late 1960s and '70s, rugby was completely woven in to my home, my friends and my family. It was just the way of life back then; to be throwing a ball around with your brother or your mates at every available opportunity; to be at the rugby club; to be involved, either directly by playing or by being there watching your team. We would all troop down to the College Rifles club every Saturday of the season, kit bags in the back, ready for anything. After the games, Mum and Dad would go upstairs to the bar where they'd have a grand old time with their mates and buddies from the club – a few drinks and a lot of banter, and I even recall the odd sing-song! All of us kids would be left to our own devices, playing in the changing rooms downstairs or we'd be out on the pitches re-enacting great rugby moments and running ourselves ragged. Just fantastic times. And then, when the evening was done, we'd all pile back into the car and Dad would drive us home and we would pick over the game, talk about the players who impressed, or analyse the mistakes that were made. It was an education and an immersion into the game that was almost total. The game of rugby was around me all the time, and it got into my blood and into my bones.

In those early days I had a very important job up at the club, something I took very seriously, a position of responsibility that required intense devotion and hard work. I was the official mascot for brother Mark's College Rifles team. Dad coached the two sides (called The Gunners and The Troopers) that the club put out at Under 10 level. Both teams were very good too; there was competition for all positions and both sides used to regularly rack up scores of 60 or 70 points against other clubs. And before the home games, even at only three or four, I would be dressed in the College Rifles kit and trot out in front of them, proud as punch, chest puffed out. I still have a photo of me as mascot in those days, with Mark's huge baggy way-too-big shorts on, and I'm holding on to what looks like a huge oversized rugby ball, and I'm clearly as happy as Larry. I absolutely loved the whole thing about running out with the team, and it must have been about this time that I recall pleading with Mum to be allowed to play, and her putting her foot down and saying it wasn't going to happen until I was five!

When I did start playing, reality kicked in. The way rugby worked in those days, you were put into a team depending upon your weight not your age. That meant that the fatter, heavier kids like me ended up playing with and against boys who were older – sometimes by two or three years. I did spend a while deluded that I would be able to play in the Number 10 position, fly-half; I could see myself as the film-star-good-looking, mercurial lynchpin, calling the shots and ghosting through half-spaces to score magnificently under the posts . . . but it seems that I shared this view alone. I was a big lump, so they put me in the front row (similar to working in a boiler room on a ship) and off I went. To use a well-worn rugby analogy, there are two types of players in a rugby team, piano movers and piano players. It was clear that my body shape meant I was never going to be one of the piano players, so I put down the music and lowered my shoulder.

Despite Dad's All Black heritage, there was no expectation forced onto myself or Mark about the level of rugby that we were going to play, so in terms of what I wanted to be, no one was forcing the issue. I can honestly not think of a single instance where I felt under pressure or expected to perform. Throughout my whole association with College Rifles as a young player, I never felt that anyone at the club treated me any differently to anyone else. None of Dad's mates, or the other grown-ups around, ever made any remarks or passed any comments that I can recall about following in Dad's footsteps or becoming an All Black some day; I was left to get on with enjoying the game that I loved playing, and I had the best of times at that club, running round like a little hooligan with the rest of the kids. I think the whole set-up was less intense and scrutinised than it is today; talent was allowed to rise to the top naturally, within a focused winning environment certainly, but also in an environment where things were kept in perspective. The game delivered much more, and was valued much more than just for the results on the pitch. The shared activity, the sense of community and the togetherness it fostered were equally valued, and I think that has changed to a degree these days. Remember too in those days there wasn't the same amount of rugby footage on TV, and the coverage of games was much less – in fact I don't think we got a colour TV until the late 1970s. So I don't think that international rugby was thought about, or talked about, or available to the extent that it is today, so it wasn't necessarily a conscious aspiration I had. I suspect that if I had a son to go with my two beautiful girls, it would be very different for him. He would be finding his way as a young player in the world today, and I suspect that the expectation on him would be massive. That would be hard to cope with. Interestingly, I am not sure that rugby ability necessarily runs in the family that often. There are probably only about 20 or so father-and-son All Black families, and only two or three families where three generations have played in the black shirt. It is a very rare thing indeed.

I played for College Rifles until school at 11, and it was then that I went to the Sacred Heart College in Auckland where I was taught and coached by Guy 'be the best that you can be' Davis. As I got a little bit older my rugby started to get a bit more focused, a bit more serious. My school rugby career progressed, and I managed (albeit unwillingly!) to let go of the fly-half dream. I continued to grow physically bigger and stronger than a lot of other boys my age, and it wasn't long before I was a regular pick in the front row for the school team. The front row refers to the front row of the scrum, which is one of the key facets of a game of rugby. If and when a mistake is made during a game, the scrum is the method used to restart the ball and get the game moving again. It is a key part of the game, and can be thought of (along with the line-out, which is how the ball is restarted when it goes off the field of play), as laying the foundations for a team's success. If your scrum is good, you're halfway home.

I enjoyed playing there, and I made a good job of it; as I came towards the last years of my school career I began to get selected for representative rugby – which means moving up a level from the school side and playing in an area or 'representative' team selected from all the school teams in the region. The deal was pretty much the same as it is today: coaches and teachers of all the teams around the country would be looking out for players who could possibly go on to the next level. They would make sure that they encouraged the players and put them forward for the trials when they came around. These trials were basically a series of sessions and games during which coaches and selectors would watch, switch players and combinations around, and then make their selection. In New Zealand, the teachers and coaches are plugged into a wide informal network of colleagues, officials, ex-players, selectors and club administrators across the country. This

We all had to make a living outside the game of rugby, whatever level we played at. It was a purely amateur sport from top to bottom; there was no real money in it – everyone involved in rugby had a day job.

informal network, these hundreds of guys giving up their time, week in week out, to coach the game, are the jungle drums of the rugby world, and there is always a particular team, or a fast-developing player, or a couple of rising stars to keep them beating. With everyone keeping their ear to the ground, any kids with potential were nudged along and watched closely.

When I went to those trial games, I was absolutely clear about what I wanted: to be selected. It wasn't in my make-up to back off or go easy or be intimidated. I was your typical young buck, full-throttle from the first whistle, getting stuck right into the opposition at every available opportunity. I may not have been working to a grand plan or long-term strategy, but I knew that my job for the next 80 minutes was to make damn sure that the guy opposite me was going to come off the pitch second best.

I knew what I wanted, and I wanted to win.

AN IDEA TO TRY: WHAT DO YOU WANT?

Write in the middle of a piece of paper, 'What do I want?' Around it, write down your answers to that question. It might be 'money' or 'good health' or 'friends' – whatever it is, put it down.

Step two is to ask yourself 'How?' How will you get 'good health'? Again, write it down. Be as specific as you can, and when you've done that, ask 'how' again'. Keep asking the how question – it unwraps the layers quickly and gets you back to specific actions that you can start to do. 'I want to be in great health. How do I do that? By eating properly and exercising more. Again, how? By setting up a more specific diet, and by putting together a programme of fitness. How can I set up a more specific diet? Well, I can start by understanding what I want to achieve by changing my diet – losing a stone of weight – and then looking at my current intake, analysing how much carbohydrate I'm taking on board and looking to find alternatives to carbs that I can substitute into my weekly shopping. With regard to my fitness, I will book a session at the gym and talk to a trainer there about putting a plan together that works for me.' And so on. It's a fact that if you know where you are going, you're more likely to get there – if you don't, you have no chance.

The more thorough you make this, the more likely it is to stick, so when you are considering these 'how' questions, make sure that you *really* think it through. Ask yourself what it will feel like when you get there. Ask yourself how you will be different when you have achieved it. Be clear about the timing – are you talking days, weeks, months, or years?

That approach to trial games turned out well. I was selected as a reserve for New Zealand at Under 16 level. I would have preferred to be the number one choice naturally, but I was still absolutely thrilled to have my own black jersey, and although the team kit consisted of white socks, I got myself a pair of the legendary black socks with the two white bands around the top. In fact, when I went out running during this time, either for training or to loosen up after a game,

I used to get a real kick out of wearing those socks, although my dad's way of thinking had clearly rubbed off on me. I'd only wear them under tracksuit pants so that no one would see them and think me arrogant! Maybe Dad's modesty hadn't transferred itself to me completely though, because occasionally – when it was dark outside and no one was likely to see me, just once or twice – I might have worn them with shorts!

Things continued to go well for me on the pitch. In 1981 I was made captain of the New Zealand Secondary Schools team. That was a definite high point of my young life. To have not just been selected, but to have also been given the honour and the responsibility of leading the team out – that was something about which I was immensely proud.

But it never happened. I never did lead that team out. It was a great shame, but larger forces were at work. South Africa were in New Zealand on tour, and their presence caused uproar.

BACKGROUND

My own personal disappointment was just a tiny footnote to a much bigger story – the 1981 tour of New Zealand by South Africa. Rugby was still a minority sport on the global stage, but that 56-day tour made headlines across the world's TV channels and newspapers. It was a politically charged time, and it was an unhappy time for all concerned – it has subsequently been tagged by political commentators as the moment when New Zealand lost its innocence. That seems a remarkably sad and far-reaching assessment, and I make no claims to know whether or not it is true, but what I can say is that it was a tour that divided the country and caused massive civil disturbance across New Zealand, and created fallout that would impact on rugby in the country for years to come. It was certainly a moment in time that perfectly illustrated the way that the game of rugby and the wider society of New Zealand are inextricably linked and intertwined.

The central issue concerned the ethics of hosting a rugby team from an apartheid-ruled country. South Africa was a pariah on the international sports scene, and as the tour dates approached, it was clear that a significant proportion of the New Zealand public were unhappy with hosting them. On the face of it, and with the benefit of hindsight, it is clearly intolerable that tacit support for a racist system of government should ever be given by welcoming the tour, but at the time, and given the long and combative history between the two countries, the rugby purists were vociferous in their assertions that rugby and politics were totally separate, and that the tour should go ahead. The government of the day also took that view, and so the tour party arrived – and from the moment they did, protests and civil disturbances erupted. This created a peculiarly polarised reaction in a significant number of rugby fans, who were adamant that a group of protestors should not be able to prevent a game of rugby taking place – and so the lines were drawn and the battle began. Police in riot gear were highly visible both at the games and outside the grounds, protestors forced their way onto pitches, rugby fans jeered and cheered as

I knew that my job for the next
80 minutes was to make damn
sure that the guy opposite me was
going to come off the pitch second
best. I knew what I wanted, and
I wanted to win.

the police cleared them away – a couple of protestors even got into a light aeroplane and dropped flour bombs onto the pitch during the last test match. In fact, there were a lot of dignified, well-ordered and non-violent protests as well. I suspect that across the country there was much debate on both sides of the argument – but debate doesn't sell, so news channels went for the big stories like the footage of protestors dressed as clowns being hit by police batons. It looked like the whole country was at war.

The immediate impact that the political unrest surrounding that tour had on me was the cancellation of the New Zealand Secondary Schools matches that were scheduled to be played. But however disappointed and frustrated I was by this, little did I know that in the years ahead, the impact of that tour on my own career would be much more far-reaching. As a result of the unrest and the political debate created in those two months, no officially sanctioned New Zealand rugby team was ever to tour to South Africa again while the apartheid regime was in power. The key words there are 'officially sanctioned team'. An unsanctioned breakaway group of All Blacks did tour there in 1986, and in so doing, gave me a golden opportunity. I'll tell you all about that a little bit later on.

In the meantime, I got over my disappointment of not leading out the schools team. I was given the award of Auckland Schoolboy Player of the Year that year. It was presented to me by future All Black Grant Fox, who was at that time an up-and-coming talent – he'd won the same award the year before. That summer I left school and started working as a builder. In those days, and as peculiar as it now sounds, we all had to make a living outside the game of rugby, whatever level we played at. It was a purely amateur sport from top to bottom; there was no real money in it – everyone involved in rugby had a day job.

The building work was physical and it kept me in great shape. The hours were 7.30 to 5 o'clock every day and you had no option but to work hard when you were on site. I needed to clock up something like 8000 hours, and four or five years' work, in order to finish my apprenticeship, and they were strict about logging hours and keeping records of what I'd done. But I was enjoying myself. I was learning a trade as well as keeping fit and strong for my rugby. For example, mixing concrete by hand was ideal conditioning for me. It built good upper body strength and contributed to the levels of stamina I needed to develop. And just like my dad, I used to run home after work. One quarter of my time in those days was spent learning joinery in a workshop, which I enjoyed greatly and was reasonably good at, but for the remainder of the time I was doing general building work, and being on site meant mixing with some real characters. It was certainly pretty earthy at times!

I still clearly recall sitting with a cynical old builder who I think should probably remain nameless. We were listening to the rest of the boys all talking about their hard drinking escapades, and the girls that they had 'entertained' the previous weekend. This guy turned to me and said, 'To be honest Sean, I'd rather have a pint of lager than make love to my wife.' And I nearly fell off my seat! I couldn't fathom how you could say such a thing – I was shocked to the core, not only because he thought like that, but also because he had actually shared it with me! I might have thought I was a man of the world, but I was still naïve in a lot of ways, and not particularly worldly. I also remember being shocked, though impressed, with the sharp practices that abounded, and I learnt a good deal about how the trade worked that you wouldn't find in any official apprenticeship manual. I think that it was in this phase of my life where I really started working out what I wanted. I had moved on, and I wanted to keep moving. I had got the bit between my teeth with regard to rugby – I was involved in representative level teams, I loved it there, I loved the socks (!) and I wanted more. But I was still young, and if truth be told I was probably a bit too cocky and self-assured. I fear that if I were able to travel back in time to point out a few things to my younger self, I wouldn't have listened! However, I have learnt a few key lessons about getting what you want.

First of all, getting what you want starts with *knowing* what you want. That may sound a little self-evident, but I am constantly surprised by people – players, businessmen, whoever – who don't have a well-formed, well-thought-through and clear picture of what they want. It is only by being absolutely clear on what is important to you and what you want that you are able to move towards it. As I mentioned before, if you don't know where you are going, any road will take you there.

AN IDEA TO TRY: KNOWING WHAT YOU WANT

'What I want' is very different to 'what I don't want'. Make sure that what you want is a positive outcome, positively phrased. 'I don't want to work in an office for the rest of my life' is a valid aspiration, but it is negatively formed. It focuses on moving *away* from working in an office and not moving *towards* anything. So make sure that you focus on what you *do* want. 'I want to work outside.'

'I want to give up smoking' is another example. Again, that is framed in the negative. Make it a 'moving towards', positive outcome – for example, 'I want to be free from addiction.' Just making this small but important change is much more likely to create outcomes that excite and motivate. What *do* you want?

But getting what you want isn't just about wishing it to be so and it just happening for you. It means having discipline, focus and stamina to keep working towards it when it seems difficult, to carry on where you might ordinarily have stopped, and to nurture the belief within yourself that it is possible. No bugger is going to deliver your dreams and aspirations for you on a plate, and to set your mind to achieving them means accepting hard work into the bargain.

Getting what you want also means that you have to be clear not only about the outcome, but also about the price that will have to be paid to get there. Is the price worth paying? Is it in line with who you are? There is a danger in setting out to get what you want at absolutely *all* costs, as Dean Richards found out to his – and his club's – cost.

Richards was the coach of Harlequins, a London-based club pursuing a place in the final stages of the rugby European Cup competition. They were in a tight, dogfight of a match against the Irish side Leinster, and in the intensity of the moment, Richards made a dreadful decision. With his specialist kicker already substituted off the pitch earlier in the match, his side needed someone to kick a drop goal to win. Because the kicker was already off the field, the only way he would be allowed to come back on would be as temporary cover for someone who had a blood injury. Players are not allowed to remain on the pitch if they have a blood injury, and a replacement can be sent on to cover for them while it is attended to – a sensible law. With time almost up, Richards ordered that a fake blood capsule be taken onto the pitch and given to one of the players. The player bit into it, faked a blood injury, and the kicker was duly allowed back on to the pitch to play the last few minutes of the game. The subterfuge was not unnoticed by Leinster, who immediately complained to match officials. Worse, the whole episode was picked up by TV cameras. In the furore that followed, Richards not only lost his job, he was also banned from any direct involvement in the game for three years. It was a heavy price to pay for knowing what he wanted, but not having thought through what was and what was not acceptable in the pursuit of its achievement. I know that Richards is genuinely remorseful for both the damage to the game and for the impact that it has had on his life and career – it was an error of judgement – but it does serve as a salutary tale of caution to us all. In the clamour to get what you want, the manner in which you do it is important too. Acknowledge that you have boundaries and lines across which you will not go – and know what these boundaries are – because in the heat of battle, or in the split second where you have to make a decision, you need to make the right call. Not all actions or decisions can be undone, and as Nelson Mandela is fond of saying, life is a circle not a straight line. It will come back to you.

But that is not to say that you have to be a saint either! Certainly

Getting what you want starts with *knowing* what you want . . . it is only by being absolutely clear on what is important to you and what you want that you are able to move towards it.

it is no bad thing to have a bit of an attitude. If you are clear about where you're going and if you're going after what you want, then it is a good thing. In the game of rugby, you do need to have a hard streak in you; you need to be a bit of a nasty bastard, and if you're not, it is a good idea to cultivate it. I was lucky in that I didn't have to cultivate it in myself. I am exceptionally competitive. Being like that means that you can be a little bit nasty in order to win, and I don't think there is anything wrong with that. In fact this is an interesting attitude difference that I notice between New Zealanders and Brits. I think the ruthless streak is something that I see at home, but sense that people up here in Britain are a bit more uncomfortable with. It doesn't sit naturally with the culture here, and I don't see it being encouraged and applauded or developed as much as I think it ought to be. The telling phrase for me is this notion of being 'a good loser'. It seems to be the default first response that kids are taught from an early age here in the UK: 'Johnny, good luck with your tennis match and don't forget, if you lose, lose gracefully.'

Another example is the Scottish rugby team. They have *never* beaten the All Blacks and I genuinely wonder if – deep down – they really do want to. If they do, then perhaps they talk themselves out of it before they even go out onto the pitch. They have lost games by 30 points and talked about playing well. It seems to me that the players are happy just to have played against the All Blacks, and that their focus is more on playing well than getting the result. I have a peer from my playing days – a highly respected Scottish international – who *still* talks about the time that they played the All Blacks in 1990 and lost. He tells me that they should have beaten us. My answer is simple: maybe so, but you didn't. Even 20 or so years later, he is still bringing it up; in fact I heard him speak at a rugby function a few weeks ago and he said – I kid you not – 'one of my greatest memories was when we almost beat the All Blacks'.

BACKGROUND

In fact, that test series against Scotland was really interesting from an All Black perspective for a reason other than that they managed to run us close. At the end of the series, in which we had definitely under-performed, the blame was directed by the selectors towards one player – the captain, a guy called Buck Shelford. He was summarily dropped, but actually there was a much deeper problem with the coach and senior players in that side. Collectively we had an attitude problem. By blaming Buck, the selectors had just papered over the cracks, and despite the 'Bring Back Buck' signs that started appearing at our games, he never played for New Zealand again. Meanwhile, the rest of us carried on pretty much as before and the coach told everyone that all was well. It wasn't. The problems would surface again, painfully, a year later at the 1991 World Cup.

To get what you want, sometimes you need to think intelligently and box clever. I heard a fantastic example of this recently. It concerned a new headmistress taking over a failing girls secondary school somewhere up in the north of England. When she arrived, the discipline was terrible. Girls used the toilets as smoking and make-up

No bugger is going to deliver your
dreams and aspirations for you on
a plate, and to set your mind to
achieving them means accepting
hard work into the bargain.

rooms, and when they'd put out their cigarettes they would re-apply their lipstick and then kiss the mirrors. Over the course of a week the mirrors would become filthy with lipstick marks, and the caretaker would have to regularly spend time cleaning them all up again. As the first term under the new headmistress progressed, the issue of the mirror-kissing became a real rubbing point with the students – it was their way of rebelling and making their displeasure of the new regime known. It didn't matter what the staff team did – the girls concerned were given detentions, were reasoned with, shouted at, they had privileges curtailed – but all to no avail, the mirrors were still being kissed. And then the headmistress had a brainwave. She collected the main culprits together and along with the caretaker, took them into the toilet block. 'Whenever you do this girls, you know that it needs to be cleaned up,' she said. The girls sniggered. 'And I thought you ought to see the work that goes into cleaning these mirrors so I have asked the caretaker along to show you.' The girls smirks turned to horror as the caretaker picked up a toilet brush, swilled it around in the toilet and then wiped the mirror clean. From that day on, no lipstick ever reappeared on the mirrors. The headmistress got what she wanted.

AN IDEA TO TRY: FIXING YOUR OUTCOME

Just like disciplining pupils, if you always do things the same way in life, you will only ever have varying levels of success. Much smarter is to fix the outcome that you want, and then try using a range of different methods and strategies to get there.

Getting what you want works if you start with the answer and work backwards. If you know what you want, then the issue becomes having clarity on what needs to be done in order to get there. What changes do you need to make? What will you need to do more of, or less of? If you carry on doing what you've always done, you'll always get what you've always had. And if what you have got is not what you want . . . then change it.

A FINAL THOUGHT ON GETTING WHAT YOU WANT

I am sure you have heard the saying 'be careful what you wish for'. Getting what you want relies on you being clear on what that is, but there is one crucial point to note before you dive in – whatever it is that you think you want, the most important test that you need to apply is about whether it 'fits' with who you are. Does it really match your sense of self? Does it feel 'congruent'? If it doesn't, then perhaps you need to think more about it, and be sure that you really are heading in the right direction.

As a young builder, at about the age of 20, I knew that I wanted to be an All Black. I also knew what needed to be done to achieve that, I knew it fitted in with my personality and I was perfectly ready for the price I'd need to pay. I was beginning to develop my sense of self, to realise that I could actually become an All Black. I was being coached by Brian Lochore with the New Zealand Under 21s and I was playing well – but I still had a bit of work to do. I was young and cocky, and probably just a bit too full of myself. If I was really going to make the step up to becoming a full All Black, I needed to hear a few home truths. I needed to receive some honest feedback – and that is certainly what happened to me. I got feedback – brutal, direct right-between-the-eyes, both-barrels feedback – and it was delivered by the massive All Black legend, Andy Haden.

THREE

GROWING THROUGH LISTENING

WHEN I WAS A YOUNG LAD, I think it is fair to say I had an opinion on everything, and my opinion of myself was pretty high. That was until I met Andy Haden.

I was part of the Under 21 New Zealand team coached by a certain Mr Brian Lochore (remember the name!), and felt like I was at the top of my game. Attending a training session with the senior Auckland side that I was now a part of, I was delighted – but a little intimidated – to be on the same pitch as the growling, towering, glowering Andy Haden. He was a huge presence, both physically and in the world of international rugby. He stood head and shoulders over most other players, wore size 13 boots, had played over one hundred times for the All Blacks . . . and he didn't do 'quiet'. A thorn in the side of the establishment, Andy wouldn't doff his cap to superiors, and he was forever having run-ins with them (just after gaining his first All Black cap, he fell out with the Auckland team selectors and buggered off to Europe to play for a season or two before returning). He didn't accept the traditional amateur status of players – he was one of the pioneers in recognising that the game needed to change. He had begun to notice that he was losing team-mates to early retirements because they could no longer afford to play senior-level rugby whilst holding down jobs and looking after young families. It was often the guys who had been around a while and who had all the experience that were cutting short their careers and sometimes, ironically, these top-flight players were announcing their retirement after matches that had just been watched by 60,000 or 70,000 paying spectators. Andy, quite rightly, took exception to this patronising and archaic view, and set about trying to change things. Perhaps above all, Andy was known to be ferociously straightforward. He didn't back down or let things go quietly. If something needed saying, or someone needed telling, Andy was your man. Whoever they were and whatever their role, they got it unpolished and honest, and I am guessing that even today there are both players and administrators who are smarting at Andy's forthright views.

The manner in which he approached the game itself was years ahead of its time. He was a battering ram, yes, but he also played with guile and cunning. He was technically excellent and studied and practised intensely – he was a real student of the game. Andy brought a pathological pursuit of excellence to his rugby that would fit in well in the modern era – and he'd have made a few dollars too.

So, here I was, still a young lad, kicking around the fringes of the senior players in the Auckland set-up, in awe of these All Blacks and just desperate not to mess up. And now, all of a sudden, here comes the big, surly, aggressive Andy Haden. He comes right up to me, points, and growls 'Get a ball. Let's do some line-outs!'

Oh God.

Here's how it works. Andy jumps up, and when he reaches his highest point, when he's at full stretch, there, as if by magic, will be the ball. He will tip the ball back with his fingertips, our scrum-half will catch it and then away we go. We have won the ball, we continue to play the game and all is good with the world.

Except that the first bit, the bit about the ball magically being there, is where I come in. As a hooker, one of my key jobs is to throw the ball into the line-out, and make sure it is there at exactly the right height, with exactly the right amount of pace on it for the big man to collect. The brutality and coordination of the scrum is in direct contrast to the deft and delicate accuracy needed to throw a ball into a line-out. You have to be able to throw the ball up to 20 yards, and thread it through a proverbial needle. Accuracy is key.

I was petrified as we walked over to the line-out practice area. I already knew that my throwing was probably one of the weakest parts of my game. Up to then, I'd been satisfied with generally putting it in the right area, and leaving the jumper to sort the rest out, but everything I knew about Andy Haden told me that unless I was spot-on, I was going to be in trouble.

The first ball was too low.

I got a mean and loaded stare, then a terse 'Higher!' from Andy, and so I prepared to do it again. They say that in football when you're about to take a penalty in a big game, it seems like the goalkeeper grows and the goal shrinks – your perspective gets distorted. Well,

Making sure you listen
to the right people – and
they're not always the
people that you like –
helps massively.

I remember feeling exactly that way as I got ready to throw my second ball into the line-out. I couldn't work out the distances, I was panicking, nervous, tense. I could feel the enmity oozing from Haden, and I could tell by the stoical heads-down approach of the other guys and the fact that they were avoiding my eye that they also knew that a potentially ugly situation was developing.

The second ball flew past, way too high.

Andy didn't take too kindly to a cocky pup who couldn't hit him where and how he wanted the ball in the line-out.

So he gave me some feedback.

He told me to fuck off.

Until I could throw the ball into the line-out properly, he told me he wasn't going to waste his time and his talent. He made me go and fetch another hooker, telling me that he was playing and I wasn't. I was substituted out for the rest of the line-out drill and I went back to the changing room and sat there in silence, thinking about what he'd said. A part of me was tempted to tell him to stick his line-out throwing, but deep down I knew that he was right. I had to confront the fact that I wasn't good enough. I wasn't up to the All Black standard that he worked to, and the simple truth was that unless I radically changed this part of my game, I was not going to achieve all that I wanted to.

So I went off and got it sorted. I went to see a guy called Kevin Boyle who taught me the finesse and technical detail I needed, and then I spent a long time practising to become the best that I could possibly be at that part of my game. When, a little while later, I went back again to have another go with Andy, I was petrified and shaking. Although I had realised the work and effort needed to be as good as he expected and demanded me to be, and even though I knew I had put that hard work in, I was still worried about whether I would be able to hit the required standard . . . but it worked out well – I made the right throws and I passed the examination. Mr Haden of course wasn't clapping and cheering and slapping me on the back as I nailed the throw time after time – a grunt and a nod at the end of the session was all I got. But that was enough. It was probably among the most understated feedback I ever received, but it meant the world to me. Andy Haden had given me straight feedback that found the mark. It had an immediate impact on me and has remained with me to this day as one of the most important bits of feedback I have ever received. I called my 1998 autobiography *Fronting Up*, and as fronting up goes, that was absolutely a pivotal moment for me. I could have continued with playing at the standard I had already achieved and been a good, solid provincial player – a big fish in a small pool – but gone nowhere internationally; however, through actively taking on board his feedback, I was stung into the realisation that actually, I wanted more. That I received such genuinely unequivocal feedback helped me immensely.

AN IDEA TO TRY: WHO CAN HELP YOU?

Think critically, be interested, ask questions. Thoughtful questions provide insight and deliver riches, and you can learn from just about everyone around you. You have to identify those people around you who can help you to grow. Look for 'models of excellence' – people that do the things you would like to do and who seem to do so with ease and naturally. Then ask them how they do it! Find out what mechanisms they use, listen closely to how they handle situations and conversations. Spend time with them, and try out the things you see them doing.

Taking feedback from the Andy Hadens of this world is important if you want to get better. Making sure you listen to the right people – and they're not always the people that you like – helps massively. One of the key ingredients for me in achieving the longevity and success that I enjoyed in rugby lay in continually seeking out the people involved in the game that I respected and that I could learn from, and then – however painful or ego-bruising it was – to try to do exactly that, learn from them.

A generally accepted observation is that one of the traits that makes people competitive and successful is drive. I would agree. People who hold an innate competitiveness and a willingness to work hard tend to approach life and its challenges with conviction and belief, and that pays dividends. However, I believe that this does come with a caveat, because to be truly successful – to reach the stage of being the best that you can be – I am convinced that you need to keep your ears open. You have to be able to take and process feedback. It pays to understand that you don't know everything. The very best players I have played with, the best coaches, the best managers I have come across in business, all of them understand the importance and value of feedback, and seek growth and development through that process. And conversely, a reasonable number of those who were less successful displayed the reverse – that of not wanting to listen to others.

Perhaps you know the old story about the highly academic professor who travelled to Japan to learn about Zen Buddhism from a Japanese master called Nan-in. When the professor arrived, he talked and talked at the master about all the things he knew, and he had a firm opinion on everything. Finally the master gently interrupted, and offered the professor tea. As he poured it, he filled the cup and kept on going so that the tea spilled all over the table. 'Stop! The cup is full!' shouted the professor. The Zen Buddhist master replied, 'Like this cup, you are full of your own opinions. I cannot put anything more in. To learn from me, you will have to empty your cup.'

I know it is an old tale, but it perfectly demonstrates this distinction that I am talking about. Thinking about myself, I suspect I was a little guilty of that when I was younger. I certainly wish that I had written down the answers to life's problems when I was a young man! I was so certain that I knew just about everything there was to know but now, some 20 or so years later, I am much less certain. Recognising that there is always more to learn, and avoiding the temptation to walk around with my cup full of my own ideas and beliefs has been important in allowing me to grow.

There are lots of people – individuals and organisations – that actively seek out a 'feedback session'. Some organisations have ingrained a culture of holding intensive 'lessons learnt' sessions after a key event – a sales victory or even a lost piece of business. But are they really listening? It is hard to keep sessions like this honest, and genuinely focused around the seeking and giving of valuable, constructive feedback. I have seen examples where businesses seek only to use such feedback to reinforce their own prejudices or view of themselves – actual real genuine feedback isn't really welcome. To 'institutionalise' the feedback loop, to write it into the way that you

It pays to understand that you don't know everything. The very best players I have played with, the best coaches, the best managers I have come across in business, all of them understand the importance and value of feedback, and seek growth and development through that process.

operate as a business or an individual, takes real commitment. You have to be very committed to the cause of hearing what you *need* to hear rather than just what you *want* to hear. And that is much harder to do than to say. In rugby there is a phrase that coaches use. They say it is important to 'practise the skill not the drill'. In other words, it isn't about going through the steps and just getting the mechanics of the process right – it is about being genuine in looking to develop the skill in question, to learn and grow and improve from what you are doing. If you don't, you're just practising the drill and not the skill – and you're missing a huge opportunity.

AN IDEA TO TRY: IF YOU'RE GOING TO LISTEN, LISTEN PROPERLY

Active listening is all about engaging with the person to whom you are talking – giving signals to show that you are listening and then actively internalising, analysing and synthesising what you are hearing. I would like to suggest that today, you take it up a notch. Listen aggressively for the day. I don't mean outwardly being aggressive, but inwardly, grab hold of everything that is being said. Shake it about. Interrogate it. Listen to the words, listen to the context and ask yourself continuously –what is really being said to me? Don't just think about the way it is being delivered – listen to the tone of voice as well. Look at the non-verbal cues that are being given. Think about what is not being said. Don't spend your time waiting for the other person to finish talking just so that you can continue making your points – take time to genuinely reflect on what is being said to you. And listen fast. Work hard; hear what is being said and internalise the information quickly, analyse it straight away, be busy all the time.

So whatever it is that you do, in order to improve you have to make sure that you go out and seek feedback, but you also have to make sure that you don't surround yourself with people who kiss your arse and don't deliver truths where they're needed. People who don't tell you the truth, even if they're motivated by compassion, are dangerous to have around if that is all you've got, because things don't get said, and issues don't get examined. You won't grow if you're not challenged.

A guy I know well and have worked for (and for whom I have a great deal of time), runs a very successful international business. He grew the brand phenomenally in a very short period of time, and for a while, he and everybody else there were riding the crest of a wave – the money was rolling in, the business was expanding exponentially, and everybody around him was happy and smiling, with no questions being asked. While the sun shone, everybody carried on cheerfully like there was no tomorrow. And he is honest enough to be able to say that looking back, he got caught up in that. He didn't have people around him who challenged him. Everyone was enjoying the ride, and there was no one questioning his, or the business's, decisions. People in the business lived the high life. They all travelled first class, money was no object, and the levels of control on spending and marketing weren't tight enough. In the end, it all got silly and had a negative impact on the business. When the market turned, the rigour and the

It is true of course that you do need to listen to others, but you do also need to listen to yourself – listen to and trust your instinct, your abilities.

tightness required to see the business through in good order were missing, and it really struggled. I think he recognises that at least in part it was of his own making. He didn't have anyone close that he trusted who could question him and his decisions, and in the end that cost him a few quid. He looks back now and recognises that far from doing harm, it does you and your business good to have challenging people around you. It is worth having people around you who keep you honest, who make you think carefully about what you're doing.

But you have to be careful about where you get your feedback from too. Young guns and dynamic graduates might keep the business or the team fresh, and they certainly bring new blood and ideas, but the flip-side is that older people in the team can also bring value in their experience and wisdom. Where you do have people who have been around the block and have seen a few things in their time, they bring a perspective to bear on the challenges and issues that younger people perhaps can't always do.

There is a particular art-form that has taken this notion of 'growing through listening to experience' and integrated the concept into the very fabric of how the medium works. I recently discovered that the Royal Ballet in London, like other ballet companies around the world, has a specific position within the Company called a Repetiteur. This is a senior and important role, and it is often fulfilled by a highly experienced ballet dancer – someone who has danced the actual ballet that is being rehearsed and who knows it inside out. Their role is to pass on the specific technical steps of the ballet, as well as giving the rehearsing dancers a direction and a feel for the emotional tone of the piece – how they should be feeling and how that feeling should be expressed when they are dancing. They spend time with the different dancers both individually and collectively and their role is about leveraging their technical expertise and experience in order to maximise the potential of the dancers. I don't know too much about the actual ballet itself – for some reason I have never excelled at dancing – but I do know that the value of having someone there who is able to give precise and highly attuned feedback must be of great value to the whole company. It seems to me that ballet has learnt, or evolved, to recognise that learning and listening from those with experience adds huge value to the enterprise.

I suppose we had something similar within the All Black set-up when I was part of it. Significantly less polished than a ballet repetiteur, but just as effective in its own way; it was the 'back of the bus' conversation. It is a fact of life that the more senior you are as a player on the tour, the further back in the bus you sit – and I am willing to bet that if you have ever been to play away games with your school, or travelled on a school bus, you will have experienced it. For those new kids and greenhorns sitting in the front seats, it is a long way back. When we were on tour, or on a long coach journey, the younger blokes who were new to the squad were, in turn, called to the back of the bus. I can tell you that however big and ugly you are, however self-confident and brash, getting that call could be a little intimidating. You had to walk back up the aisle, with sarcastic comments and good-natured ribbing from all the boys along the way. Right at the back, the old lags would be sitting in their fiefdom, arms folded, nodding you towards a vacant seat in the corner. Once there, the older guys gave you a bit of a hard time, and then they got all serious. They talked to you about what being an All Black means – the tradition, duty, and responsibility that comes with selection; the standards of behaviour, the ethics and the values that set an All Black apart. To be called to the back of the bus, and then to be sitting among the senior players (many of whom you have looked up to and respected for years as you made your own way in the game), while they talked to you about such weighty matters was a powerful thing. I am sure that in these days of sports psychology it might seem a bit old hat and amateur, but it was an All Black tradition that stood the test of time for many years and one that I believe contributed significantly to the success of the team. I hope they still do it.

To be the best that you can be, you need to listen to the feedback you are getting, because you never know where the pearl of wisdom is going to come from. It was at the back of a bus that I heard a senior player saying, 'Once an All Black, always an All Black. It doesn't stop when you retire.' That struck me at the time as a particularly useful way to think, and it has stayed with me ever since. However, the point I want to make is that I wasn't even involved in the conversation – I was just listening in while some young bloke was getting the once-over. But it stuck with me as a way I wanted to live my life . . . and it underlines the fact that if you are listening, you can learn from some surprising and unexpected places. You need to be willing to listen, willing to hear. Of course, that doesn't mean that you have to take everyone's advice and feedback 'on board' as people are fond of saying these days (that would be difficult and you'd probably end up having a nervous breakdown trying to be all things to all men) but keep your ears open, because just one piece of feedback, intentional or otherwise, positive or negative . . . if it is the right piece of feedback, it can unlock a whole puzzle.

I know of a great example shared with me by a friend of mine; true story. Kate was a highly successful marketing professional for an international company. She worked exceptionally hard, putting in long hours, and was seemingly happy in what she was doing.

Keep your ears open, because just one piece of feedback, intentional or otherwise, positive or negative . . . if it is the right piece of feedback, it can unlock a whole puzzle.

However, her entire life and career changed when a colleague said to her in passing, 'You know, we can always rely on you for a negative comment, Kate.' It was only a throwaway line said in the midst of a fast-moving meeting, but that comment hit her hard. The more she reflected on the comment, the more she realised that it was true, that she was in a perpetual negative frame of mind. And she didn't like the idea that this was how she had turned out, so in the following weeks and months she re-evaluated everything to do with her life – the long hours, the tetchy meetings, the stress . . . and she stopped it all. She gave up her big marketing job, she sold her house, went back to college and re-trained as a life coach . . . and now she leads the kind of life she had always wanted to, but had somehow lost sight of somewhere along the way. Kate wasn't looking for feedback, but she listened when it came her way.

AN IDEA TO TRY: LISTEN TO YOURSELF

An observation that I have made is that there are people who have natural ability and talent but who doubt it, primarily just because it seems to come too easily. If it comes easy, the thought process goes, it can't be right! It is true of course that you do need to listen to others, but you do also need to listen to yourself – listen to and trust your instinct, your abilities. If everybody is turning left but you think you should be turning right, then be brave enough to back yourself. Turn right! It is very easy to undervalue yourself and not put enough faith or trust in your own abilities and judgement. Don't. Back yourself every time. Listen to your own heart or instinct or gut feel or whatever you want to call it. While the outside world is clamouring for your attention and shouting 'Zig!' at you, take care to listen to the voice inside you that is saying 'Zag!'

A FINAL THOUGHT ON GROWING THROUGH LISTENING

Growing through listening means that you have to pay attention, you have to be curious and you have to actively look for experiences that you can learn and grow from. The biggest barrier to that happening is when we close our ears, stop listening, and think that we have all the answers. If I have to think about one moment which I am most thankful for when I look back on my career, I think in many ways I would have to pinpoint the Andy Haden incident. I think that was probably the moment when I began to realise that I wasn't perfect, and that I had to listen and learn. It was the starting point of a new set of targets and aspirations for me, and after growing up and playing rugby by relying on my natural size and strength, it was the point at which I decided to actively and aggressively manage my own abilities. What I subsequently achieved can, in my mind at least, be traced back to Mr Haden telling me to fuck off.

FOUR

BEING A TEAM PLAYER

IN THE SEASONS THAT FOLLOWED, my desire to listen and learn improved, and so did my playing. My increased accuracy in the line-outs started to pay dividends and I began to think about and develop the rest of my game in the same way. I knew that Brian Lochore, the coach of the national senior side, was keeping an eye on my progress, and when in 1986 many of the senior players were unavailable for the upcoming test match against France, I wondered if I would get the call to the only team I wanted to be a part of.

BACKGROUND

The bigger rumblings of international politics continued to impinge on the world of rugby. In 1985, South Africa was supposed to host the New Zealand All Blacks, but a couple of lawyers dug through the New Zealand Rugby Union constitution and made a legal challenge. They contended that touring apartheid South Africa would be in contravention of the constitution. The ruling went in their favour, and the tour was cancelled.

This incensed the rugby purists, those same people who had supported the 1981 tour and so, under the management of Colin Meads, the All Black legend, a team was put together that included 28 out of the 30 players selected for the cancelled 1985 tour and the following year they went to South Africa anyway. It was an unofficial, non-sanctioned tour, but with so many of the current All Blacks playing, it certainly had the look and feel of an All Black tour. 'The Cavaliers', as they were called, were reported to have been paid handsomely for breaking away from their union, and in those amateur days I am unsure if this was the case, that it influenced individuals to tour, but it left the New Zealand RFU with a real headache. With so many senior players ignoring their direction, and a World Cup – in fact the first World Cup in 1987 – just around the corner, the administrators had to make a decision. On the Cavaliers' return, would the union just roll over and let them rejoin the official All Black set-up and carry on as if nothing had happened, or would they need to punish them with some sort of playing ban?

The answer to the latter was 'probably', and the general con-
sensus back in New Zealand was that the team needed to be
reprimanded, and some sort of sanction brought to bear. And
that got me thinking. If they were to be punished, who would
pull on the coveted black jersey to represent New Zealand in
the scheduled one-off test against France? When the Cavaliers
returned from South Africa, the New Zealand RFU banned the
participating players for two tests. It wasn't a huge sanction,
but it sent the right signal. Punishment was due, but with the
1987 inaugural Rugby World Cup just around the corner, it was a
pragmatic and sensible ban that would show who was in charge,
but still allow the All Blacks to at least have a fair crack at the
competition.

In fact, Brian Lochore did make the decision to put out a team of
relative youngsters against the French. That team became known as
the Baby Blacks, and of the fifteen that eventually started, ten of us
were making our debuts. Yes, you'll have noticed the word 'us' in
there! Selected – although originally on the bench as reserve hooker
– for the All Blacks against France was one bursting-with-pride S.B.T.
Fitzpatrick, All Black number 871. Brian Lochore had watched me
develop as a player and decided to give me the nod on the bench.
Whether it was a case of 'better the devil you know' I am not sure – I
do know that there weren't many other options for him at the time
– but one thing I am certain about is that when the original choice
hooker got injured and Brian told me I would be starting (which
he did only on the day before the game), I was determined to grab

the opportunity in both hands. Of the two first-choice hookers who usually played in my position, Andy Dalton was banned and also recovering from a broken jaw that he picked up on the tour (courtesy of a little Bok hospitality I am sure!), and Hika Reid was also banned. I knew that getting back the All Black Number 2 jersey was going to be both of their top priorities once the two-match bans had been served. I had to make the most of this opportunity while I had the chance.

My family and Bronnie were delighted for me and I was so pleased to see them all so happy and excited about my selection. In fact, this joy and support was to be a constant throughout my playing days, and was one of the best aspects of my career. My family really enjoyed me playing for the country and they all telephoned me before every match I ever played. My dad hugged me and shook me warmly by the hand, and just for a second I thought I saw a tear in his eye as he told me he knew I would do the jersey proud. Looking back I can see now that out of everybody around me, it was Dad who understood most completely both the honour, but also the responsibility that becoming an All Black carried. He had been there and done it. His belief and faith in me were deeply satisfying, but I also knew that Dad still carried scars with him from his playing days and that playing for the All Blacks was, at times, tough. Dad was acutely aware that I had been given my chance in circumstances that meant the team I was playing in was perceived by many as one that was going to struggle – even the Baby Blacks name suggested we weren't quite ready for it – and he knew as keenly as anyone that a losing All Black has no place to hide and that in New Zealand losing a test match stays with you forever.

Although he played 27 times for the All Blacks, even all those years later, Dad still smarted at losing to the French and the Welsh.

It doesn't matter what the specific team is of which you are a part; having a clear view on where you want to get to as a team   a clear view that everyone understands and that everyone buys into – is critical to its success.

He still found it difficult to talk about, and he carried the cold fury of frustration with him to the end. Even when he was invited to come to Cardiff with the 1989 All Black tour of Ireland and Wales, my dad refused to go, and my mother had to attend instead! I bet a few of the Welshys must have thought that Fitzy Senior had gone a bit strange in his old age, refusing a great trip like that! But Dad never went back to Wales; he refused to, because he played in a losing side there and it still hurt him.

Funnily enough, that same Wales game came back to me again not too long ago, not long after my dad passed away. I was eating out in Bray, near where I live in England, and a bloke called Alan Peterson came up to me and said that he was pleased to meet me, and that he had something for me. Intrigued, I agreed to meet him a couple of weeks later, and when he turned up, he presented back to me the jersey my father wore against the Welsh on the day he lost. Alan had bid and won it in a rugby auction, and had hung it in his box at Cardiff, but when he saw me, thought I might like to have it as a memento of my dad. It was a genuinely touching gesture, and as a fair swap I gave him one of my jerseys, but after I'd thanked him and got in the car to drive home I found myself grinning, thinking about my dad, knowing full well that after losing to Wales in it, my dad would have been happy never to have seen that bloody jersey again.

I was determined that he, my family, and the country at large would not be let down by either me personally, or by the Baby Black team that was expected to turn up and lose valiantly against the mercurial French. As a team we had a crystal clear target to aim at. Forget the future, the longer-term plans and the dreams we all harboured. For now, only the French match mattered. We had to turn up and play the way the All Blacks play: tough, uncompromising rugby that would deliver a win. It was a shared view that didn't need to be thought about. We were a *team*. More than that, we were the All Blacks.

It doesn't matter what the specific team is of which you are a part; having a clear view on where you want to get to as a team – a clear view that everyone understands and that everyone buys into – is critical to its success. You have to be absolutely persistent and obsessive about what you are doing, and so unless everyone knows the plan and is totally committed to getting there, you sell yourself short. In my recent years working as a consultant to organisations to help them develop effective teams, I have come across businesses – even big, successful ones – where whole portions of their population, their team, were disengaged from the mission . . . or even not entirely sure what the mission was in the first place. Having a clarity of outcome is critical.

Equally critical and linked to this is my belief that you have to create the very highest expectation within the group. To be truly successful you have to set the standards as high as possible, and then expect everybody to consistently achieve them. And perhaps the single most important element about being a team player is to understand that you have a personal responsibility to your team and your team-mates. You have to make a personal and genuine commitment that you will do all that you can to strive to deliver those high expectations, every second of every day. Only then can you expect the same of everybody else around you. I think Jonny Wilkinson, the English Number 10, is a perfect example of this. He has an obsessive streak which means that week in, week out, over a period of years, he has continually spent extra hours practising, refining, developing, working and growing. He gives the impression that every waking hour he spends is concerned with setting and achieving the very highest standards possible.

People can get too wrapped up in the wrong things when talking about teams, but from what I have seen and learnt, position A, first base, top of the list . . . you have to do things to the very best of your ability all the time. As an individual, you cannot *not* contribute to the team. Everything that you do and say (and those things that you don't do or don't say) will impact upon the collective whole and you need to be acutely aware of that. You have an impact on the team because you're part of it – and it is you who chooses whether you want to be a positive or negative influence. If you complain, cut corners or take the easy option, or perhaps spend a good deal of time telling people how hard you are working and just how tough your life is, then don't be surprised when in the heat of battle, just when you need it most, you discover that the team has no backbone. And you shouldn't be surprised, because through your actions you have contributed to the situation. However tough it gets, whatever the issues that exist, be the best that you can be. Make sure that personally, you model the excellence you are searching for collectively. You need to be what you want the team to be, and if everyone is doing the same thing as you, then the team becomes stronger.

AN IDEA TO TRY: BUILDING A TEAM

In building your team, first of all ensure that you have a clear vision and that everybody in the team understands what it is – and equally importantly that they buy into it, that they understand where and how they are going to be expected to con-tribute, and that they are absolutely on board. No passengers, no whingers. You may well need to handle difficult team members or deal with difficult situations, in which case you should adopt the 'belly not back' approach. Talk directly, not behind their backs. Put it on the table, sort it out. But recognise too that building a team involves encouraging – in fact seeking and welcoming – diversity. As I said earlier, 'Yes men' are dangerous. You have to be okay with different people having different maps of the world, so long as they are pulling in the same direction. Expect nothing less than the very best from yourself, and those around you. Commit to the cause.

The Rolling Stones are a great example of this. To all of us looking from the outside, they're a rock group, a band. It is all just rock 'n' roll and booze and girls and partying. But in fact that couldn't be further from the truth. As one of the longest established bands in the world, they've become an exceptionally tight team, and they work hard at it – even now when the temptation must be to coast along just a little bit. When they've finished playing on a new tour, they don't hit the bars or throw televisions out of hotel windows. Instead, they collect themselves, shake hands with the key players – sponsors, VIP guests and so forth – and then they play back the entire show. They review the sound, the lighting, the set list, the musicianship . . . they look critically and in fine detail at every aspect of their performance in order to find small improvements for the next night. Rock 'n' roll, but with rigour. It doesn't matter whether or not you like their music, you have to admire their obsessive attention to detail and the high expectations that they set themselves.

Everything that you do and say (and those things that you don't do or don't say) will impact upon the collective whole and you need to be acutely aware of that. You have an impact on the team because you're part of it.

Time and time again we see the same lesson; that competent people can become extraordinary through hard work and application. Good rugby players or footballers or rock stars or businessmen and women – all of them can achieve outstanding things if they focus on being the best that they can be, and if they are in a good environment, with a good team. And it is certainly true that this mindset isn't just an individual thing, it is a collective thing as well. You and I both know that even if each individual plays to their potential there is still this unknown, unquantifiable element that kicks in when a team is really humming. I despise the phrase 'in the zone' but I understand what it means exactly. Whenever I felt it on a collective level with the All Blacks and we were absolutely humming, we knocked the stuffing out of anything that was daft enough to come up against us. Every single one of us, players and coaches, everyone was on top of their game or their job, and we nailed it. Collectively, we were being the best that we could be and it was a good feeling.

But such matters were still the stuff of dreams for me when I took the field against the French. I was winning my first cap and I was delighted that, after a tough game, we beat them. I played okay, and was retained in the team to play against Australia a little more than a week later. It was there that I came up against a bloke called Tommy Lawton, the Australian hooker, and he gave me a dreadful afternoon. He ground me into the dirt all game, and spent every second he could telling me that I wasn't good enough, and asking me what I was doing on the same pitch as him. 'You should be at home with your mother, boy,' he snarled. 'You're just a bloody baby.' That was a moment I'll never forget, but as well as intimidating me, it fired me up. If I wanted to continue to play in this team, I was going to have to step up another gear. I was worried about whether I had another gear, but I was going to give it a bloody good go.

With so many new players to work with in the Baby Blacks, Brian Lochore had a real challenge on his hands, but he was confident and made the team feel good about being part of the adventure. In international rugby, the margins between success and failure are small, and success is often about identifying small specific areas of improvement or cohesion that will make the difference. While coaching at the junior and emerging levels of rugby is all about giving players structure and shape, at the highest levels I believe that the very best coaches provide a framework within which players and teams can express themselves. Often players' technical skills are strong (although of course in constant need of attention to keep them there) but the issue of confidence and motivation become vitally important. I have seen it so many times, where a team generates a momentum and an aura of invincibility around itself that is greater than the sum of the parts. It is in this dark art that the greatest coaches excel. Good coaches – or team leaders – are a special breed.

In the following months leading up to the Rugby World Cup, I was playing well, but I'd been dropped after the Australia game. To my detriment, but New Zealand's delight, Andy Dalton was back from injury and was playing well, and the Cavaliers had all come back into the frame after serving their two-match bans. Dalton was nominated as captain for the World Cup campaign and I was selected once again as chief bench-warmer. I knew that this would mean limited game time in the competition, but I was delighted to still be involved in the set-up and I continued to work as hard as I could. Then the same thing happened that got me a starting place against the French – the guy ahead of me got injured. Andy Dalton's hamstring went just before the start of the competition, and so I began the tournament in the starting line-up. By the time he had recovered, I was settled in the side, things were going well and the management decided to keep me in the team. As it turned out, poor old Andy didn't get a run-out all tournament, and we saw off France in the final to win. At the age of 23, and on a fast, fortuitous trajectory into international rugby, I had the privilege of playing in a World Cup-winning team.

BACKGROUND: INAUGURAL RUGBY WORLD CUP, 1987

New Zealand went into the World Cup on home soil with a fragile confidence. They had beaten, and then been beaten by France the previous November, but leading up to the opening game against Italy, there was a real sense of belief in the team and training was going well. Italy were swept aside 70–6 by an All Black team that purred like a well-oiled machine. They carried on the form by beating Fiji 74–13 and then completed the Group stage by beating Argentina 46–15 to set up a quarter final against Scotland. This sterner test was passed by the All Blacks, who won it 30–3, and after going on to beat Wales in the semi-final by 49–6, they came up, once again, against the French. The final was played at a breakneck pace, and under the leadership of David Kirk, the diminutive All Black captain, the New Zealand team powered to a 29–9 victory. New Zealand went mad with joy.

Think of your team as a family. If a team feels like a family, it performs like a family, and that is a powerful, powerful thing . . . families rally round when it gets tough. Families help each other out. Families give straight counsel, and honest feedback. It is the best model I know for a successful team.

I look back now on that team, and the other successful teams that I have been a part of, and common themes emerge. You always find a few 'characters', I believe the phrase is. There is the joker – someone who takes the mickey, who provides the laughs and the light relief. They have to know when to do it and when to shut up of course – cracking gags five minutes before you go out to represent your country isn't the smartest thing to do, but having someone around the place making people laugh and putting a smile on everyone's face – they're worth their weight in gold. We also had a lazy guy in the team. I don't want to tell you who it was, because (a) it would be improper of me to do so, and (b) because I don't want to have to pay for a lawyer, but anyway I seem to recall that we had to spend a *lot* of time getting on his case, telling him 'pull yourself together, boy, get out here and train'. That is the beauty of a well-functioning team; it supports and pushes.

There are teams within teams too. Everywhere you look on a rugby pitch there are smaller units that have to work together to contribute to the whole. And life is the same. Perhaps I'm indoctrinated in the concept of the team, but as I see things they're all around us. If you define a team as a group of people working together on the same side for the same objective, we are surrounded by teams at work and play. I even refer to my family as Team Fitzpatrick, and in the same way that I drew strength and direction from my All Black colleagues, so do I from Bronnie and the girls. When you go to work and you're having a shitty day, who (I hope) is there to pick you up? Your team. You need people around you who will give you feedback and support. You need to be able to sit down and talk things through, and hear things to get you thinking. You need guys who you can trust, and who you know will be watching your back.

AN IDEA TO TRY: YOUR TEAM

Who is in your team? Who are those people around you who are involved in your performance in some way? Identify them. It might be your mum, your sister, your best friend, your mates, colleagues at work, an old teacher of yours from years back who stays in touch – anyone who is positively contributing to your development, who cheers you on, who wants you to be successful, is on your team. When you've got the list, first of all, I think you should acknowledge them. Understand the value that they have already brought in terms of how they've helped and supported you, and let them know that you see it and value it. Then take the next step – think about how to use their talents and support to even better effect. What could they do more of or less of? What changes would you need to make in order to allow them to do that? You have a resource around you and by thinking carefully about where and how to use it to best effect, you maximise the benefit of your team.

Teams need time to grow and become efficient too. As the Baby Blacks we won our first game, but the roles within the team weren't defined or clarified – we busked it a little bit on that day. Genuine understanding within a team is something that happens when a side has been playing and living and working together over a sustained period of time. Talent – sometimes unrecognised – exists within a team, and in a good team, these talents will bubble up and be used and taken advantage of. Time and time again I have seen that this is absolutely true – if the environment is right and the people within the team are right then leaders and specialists emerge. Not everyone can step up to the plate, and in fact you don't want to have all chiefs and no Indians, but those that do show leadership, and the ability to motivate a team and generate momentum by their words and actions are to be prized. They are your rocks and are incredibly valuable when the chips are down.

On the reverse side of that same coin, allow no passengers and no whingers. When I go to war I know who I would want in my team; I know who I want around me. Whether it's a rugby game or a business crisis, the same holds true. Some people step forward and contribute, while others hide, snipe, bitch and moan. Make a note of the guys that weren't there, and at the very first available opportunity, unload them. To be truly successful as a team you have to remove anything that is in danger of getting in the way of success. Whether that is a plan, a process, or a person, if it is not helping the cause, it is getting in the way. Get rid of it. You have to be ruthless sometimes.

In a team environment you don't have to like everybody but you have to respect everyone. If someone is pissing you off, you move away; unless by moving away you hurt the team in some way. If that is the case, or if you believe that there is a degree of disrespect or dishonesty, then you are morally beholden to your team-mates to have it out and get it sorted. Your team is like your family, and while just as in a family you do have to make allowances and compromises for the greater good, sometimes you need to say uncomfortable things that need to be said. Remember that All Black phrase I mentioned earlier, 'belly not back'? That puts it beautifully. If something needs to be said, don't kid yourself that ignoring it will be okay, because the chances are that it won't be. All you do by not dealing with it is make it harder to resolve in the future. Pull your boots on and have the chat.

AN IDEA TO TRY: THE TEAM AS A FAMILY

Think of your team as a family. If a team feels like a family, it performs like a family, and that is a powerful, powerful thing. A family has doings and sayings, signs and secrets. These shared values are what binds them together. Families rally round when it gets tough. Families help each other out. Families give straight counsel, and honest feedback. It is the best model I know for a successful team. This is where true competitive advantage comes from – not just from diplomas and degrees or hierarchy and the blind pursuance of goals, but from sharing, and belonging. The best teams I have been a part of drive each other hard, demand the best, and at the same time stop to pick up those who need it. Knowing that you have a team, a family who believes in you, and in whom you believe, gives you security, confidence and drive. The more that you can think of your team as your family and act (and demand that they act) as such, the more powerful I believe your team will be.

Even if each individual plays to their potential there is still this unknown, unquantifiable element that kicks in when a team is really humming . . . whenever I felt it on a collective level with the All Blacks and we were absolutely humming, we knocked the stuffing out of anything that was daft enough to come up against us.

A FINAL THOUGHT ON BEING A TEAM PLAYER

Working for something bigger than just yourself, working *together* towards a goal, is motivating and energising. It is easy to get focused just on what you want, what your own personal goals are, and to lose sight of the fact that the sense of community, team spirit and achievement that can be gained by being part of something larger than yourself is immense. Whatever your personal circumstance, finding a team (or teams) that you can commit yourself to gives huge rewards and satisfaction. It could be to do with work, family, a sports team, music, in fact pretty much anything, but whatever it is, I hope that you find, or have found, yours. If you have, you will know the rewards it brings in terms of belonging, satisfaction and the sheer joy of sharing success with others.

During the late 1980s I felt that I had found my team, and my place in the world. I was lucky enough to be part of a high-performing international rugby team . . . although if I am honest I think I probably took it for granted at the time. I didn't appreciate just how special and cohesive the group of players I belonged to really was. I was just enjoying my game, and it seemed to me that so long as we kept doing what we'd been doing, we'd stay on top of the world forever. I played hard certainly, but I was increasingly aware of my status as an All Black and a World Champion. I was only 25, and I was thoroughly enjoying the trappings of success; the accolades, and the celebrity. I began to believe that just being an All Black made me, us, invincible.

There was another lesson just around the corner.

FIVE

EMBRACING THE FEAR OF FAILURE

THE RUGBY WORLD CUP VICTORY in 1987 was achieved by an All Black team that had been rushed through its development because of the Cavalier tour to South Africa and the subsequent ban imposed on the returning players. What it meant was that we had just a year to build our team, our playing style, our balance and our focus. It was almost too quick for us to have time to worry about failure – but worry we did. We couldn't allow ourselves to fail, and both individually and collectively we turned that fear of failure into an urgency, a focus and a momentum that ultimately drove us on to success. I am not recommending this approach in the modern game though; these days the development of the perfect international team takes time. The head coach and his team have to develop a strategy, look for both current and future players who have the potential to play the type of game the coaches want and that the team can work with, and then they have to set about making it all happen. I am sure you will appreciate the lengths that coaches go to in order to get a team playing exactly the way they want: huge amounts of planning, analysis and discussion on building effective playing patterns takes place before the team even gets on to the paddock. It's the same with any competitive or commercial environment; you're working out how to maximise the talents and advantages that you have in order to get the win. And it is all about the win.

Even if it was just you and me having a running race, once around the track, the same principle applies. You would have to decide how you wanted to manage the race in order to beat me. Will you go flat out and try to leave me for dead? Or will you turn the screw from the gun, starting at a good pace and then going faster and faster to try to break me? Or perhaps you would let me take the lead and then use your superior finishing speed to outsprint me to the line. You might even, if you were truly desperate and lacking a moral compass, resort to spiking my food so that I get a bad bout of food poisoning that might negatively affect my performance . . . but whatever your strategy, you would be clear on what it was, and then you would look to execute it as efficiently as possible. In essence that is all that a rugby coach – or any coach/manager/team leader – is doing: looking at the players he's got and the plan in his mind, and then coaching that in to make sure it happens on the day. I'm not trying to be smart or patronising here, because I know it sounds awfully simple; but in reality it is. Or at least the theory is. In fact these days the entire process of getting a team to where they need to be to compete as effectively as possible can take years. Rugby is a bloody hard game too, and people pick up knocks and injuries, so should the need arise you have to prepare a good number of extra players ready to go, in order to slot seamlessly into the system you are developing. It is because of all these factors that an international rugby team's performance goes up and down in cycles. It is really hard to achieve and then sustain peak performance over a period of years, and the first Rugby World Cup signalled a real change in the way that the game was played and structured; most noticeably of all, it has had a huge and permanent impact on that cycle. Pretty much every international team now recognises that every four years they have to be at their absolute peak in terms of performance. Fear of failure at the World Cup has come to dominate the game.

Teams almost didn't want to be at their playing peak in say Year Two, because in Year Four, when the next World Cup came around, they would more than likely be on the downward slope, tired and off the pace. Fear of failure on the world stage makes that unacceptable to coaches and unions and spectators alike.

Players are still urged to only look at the next game, while coaches are now expected to manage four-year strategic plans. For the top teams, and for New Zealand in particular, it is the 'we must not, cannot fail in four years' time' strategy. And I am not convinced that this is a healthy development. I have a firm, if somewhat simplistic, belief that you should play your best team all the time, whether in Year One or Year Four; you win every game today with your best players, and tomorrow looks after itself. The game of rugby is a complicated, ferocious blend of science, war and art. (Cliff Morgan – a founding father and revered high priest of the Welsh rugby dynasty defined rugby as the perfect mix of ballet, opera, and murder. Brilliantly put.)

Deep down we knew that we
had been the architects of
our own downfall. We had
the best players, but
the worst team.

Structure and planning need to sit alongside insight and spontaneity, not on top of them, and when the whole four-year cycle is planned out to the nth degree on a spreadsheet, that is a hard balance to achieve.

However, the All Black team that I was part of in the late 1980s had no such misgivings about life and the future of rugby. It was all very simple. There had only been one World Cup, and we had won it. After that, we didn't think that failure was an option. In the following couple of seasons we played some terrific rugby and we turned over all-comers. We beat Australia repeatedly. Wales, Japan, Argentina and France were all put to bed. We beat Ireland in Dublin, and the Barbarians in London. Club teams certainly couldn't live with us, and national teams couldn't better us either on tour or at home. Each game we stepped out on to the pitch knowing that we were going to win. But as this went on match after match, there was a small nagging in the back of my mind. When would this streak come to an end? Would I be the one to let the team down? I was feeling, for the first time in years, a weight of expectation and *a fear of failure*, and that feeling was spreading through the team. When we finally did lose in 1990 to Australia in Wellington, it hurt deeply at the time, but in terms of team development it was a good thing for us. We could finally move the focus on from everyone talking about our undefeated status and wondering how long it would last, and get back to focusing on the matches themselves and our individual and collective performances. I think that in that period of time when we were winning game after game, the fear of failure had become debilitating, restrictive and having it removed – through the very act of losing – oddly put us back on the winning track.

But stupidly, we didn't learn our lesson about recognising the fear of failure and harnessing it as a positive force. We just put the episode behind us and marched on, confident that when 1991 came around, we'd turn up and win the Webb Ellis trophy again at the next World Cup. We knew that we had the best players. No doubt, position for position we were the boys to beat. But we were missing that vital ingredient of fearing failure. Not that it was totally absent, it never is if you are an All Black, but it was certainly not a driving force, and that lack of fear led to complacency, and with that I believe came the seeds of defeat.

The key 1991 World Cup match was in the semi-final stages against one of the old enemies, Australia. The Australian team and the All Blacks couldn't have had a more contrasting build-up to the game. While they went out and about in Dublin, marching up Grafton Street meeting the punters and having a good time, we kept ourselves at a distance, maintaining what we thought to be a professional and detached air. We said little, and projected pride and certainty in our mission through a steely, silent determination. Or so we thought. In fact, we just looked arrogant. The Aussie approach meant that the Irish took them to their hearts immediately and backed them instead of us – and it made a difference to the noise in the stadium, that's for sure. I cringe a little bit now when I think of us in the All Black camp, aloof and distant, coming off the coach with our game faces on and wearing suits and sunglasses.

We lost by 10 points. We were out of the World Cup. We had failed. We had been too cocky, too confident . . . and we had lost the match because the fear of failure – a driving force behind All Black rugby – hadn't been there to spur us on until it was way too late. It was one of the most deflating, difficult moments of my career and it signalled that, along with the whole team and coaching staff, we had some serious reflection and self-analysis to do. It was time for us to be honest with ourselves because we had come up short, and because we had to take responsibility. We took a lot of flak back at home, and deep down we knew that we had been the architects of our own downfall. We had the best players, but the worst team.

AN IDEA TO TRY: FEAR OF FEEDBACK

Don't be frightened of feedback. If you get feedback – either directly or insinuated – that people don't think you're up to the job, that you don't have the capability, or that specific elements of your performance were sub-standard, you have two choices. The first option is to ignore them. Which of course we both know is not really an option at all. The smarter option – the only option in fact – is to listen to what they're saying and to draw resolve from it. Set your jaw, steel yourself for a fight and with every ounce of strength throw yourself into proving them wrong, setting things right. The key is to understand the fact that there is a world of difference between fear of feedback or of failure, and harnessing that fear to positive effect.

A little while ago now I was involved as the presenter of a TV programme called *Etched in Black*. The programme set about interviewing a large number of retired, well-respected All Blacks to hear their views on the game. I had the privilege of sitting and listening to a number of great players; it was an honour to spend time with them, and interestingly they all kept raising the same three issues about being a successful All Black. First of all, they talked about the responsibility that it brought. In the same breath they also generally talked about how lucky they were to have had the talent and/or opportunity to pull the black jersey on. And then finally, almost to a man, they talked about the fear of failure. The notion of letting down their team-mates, their country and themselves was a consistent theme. The idea that while they wore the All Black jersey, they were driven by those behind them in the pecking order to keep improving – they were determined not to let anyone take it off them. Those great players whose exploits have become the stuff of fable in New Zealand talked intensely and movingly about how fear played such a large part in their success. They used fear as a motivator.

AN IDEA TO TRY: WHO IS YOUR NUMBER 2?

Who is there that is ready to jump into your boots if you drop the ball or mess things up. Take a look at them in the same way that I looked at Warren Gatland sitting on the bench match after match, test after test. He is a nice guy but I was buggered if he was having my jersey. That thought kept me out on the training pitch after the others had finished training to throw a few more line-out balls. That thought – that fear of losing my jersey to him – drove me to be tougher on myself, push harder and work more intensely than would otherwise have been the case. Who is your Warren Gatland? Find them, and feed the fear!

Structure and planning
need to sit alongside
insight and spontaneity,
not on top of them.

There is a *crucial* difference between embracing the fear of failure as against accepting failure itself. If you choose to accept failure as the normal state of affairs, you're letting yourself down; instead, much smarter is to accept that failure exists, but then set your mind, body and spirit towards ensuring that when it visits your door, as it inevitably will, you are ready and prepared to handle it effectively. It means being driven by the fear of failing, but not passively accepting it when it looks like it is coming along. By not recognising failure as an option, you are deluding yourself, and equally by not embracing and managing it, you can become debilitated. To just believe that you have to turn up to take the spoils is nonsense, but equally to want something so badly and to be frightened of not achieving it does bad things to your psyche and ultimately your performance. It can prevent you from achieving precisely the thing about which you are so worked up about: winning. This is where the idea about embracing the fear of failure comes in. You need to think about what the fear of failure does to you individually and collectively and you need to accept it as part of the process, and work out how to deal with it.

If you have failed, you might have done absolutely everything wrong. If so, there is a big lesson in there for your planning and perception – you have some serious work to do. But many times, it is by degrees and inches that we fail; small margins and individual decisions that had a telling negative impact. However, there may also be a lot of things that you did *right*, and one of the keys to using failure and harnessing it in a useful way is to be able to dig the good out of a bad situation.

There is a little story about a boy who is taken to a farm for the day, and he disappears off into the stable. When his mum finds him some time later he is still inside the stable, up to his neck in manure, wading and digging through it with his bare hands. The stench is overpowering. When his horrified mum asks him what on earth he thinks he's doing, he smiles and replies, 'Well, with all this horse shit about, there *must* be a pony in here somewhere.' It may well be that there is no pony at all, but still, it's a good outlook, and likewise you need to examine every corner of the pile of shit that is your failure and check, just in case. If you can pick ponies out of it – lessons or specifics that will help you next time – then it is a valuable exercise. However, the trick is to park it quickly – there is no value in wading around in shit forever. Learn what you can from it, then get out. Move on. Easier said than done sometimes, I know, but possible.

AN IDEA TO TRY: USING FAILURE

Aim to win. If you do win, park it quickly. If you don't, use the failure. Take a positive out of it wherever you can. Reframe it not as a failure, but as feedback, as a necessary part of the process of winning. Sometimes failing is the only thing that will allow you to win at a later date. You choose how you react to the failure. If you learn from it, the results can be powerful and can make you stronger. If you fail, don't lock it away and pretend it didn't happen. Put it on the table and have a good hard look at it while it is still fresh and still hurting. Recall what happened, play it over in your mind, brood on it. Remember what it feels like. And then promise yourself that you never, ever, want to feel like that again.

Be careful that you don't
end up believing that it is
the taking part that counts.
It isn't. It is the winning
that counts.

Recently I listened with interest to Lord Sebastian Coe talking about the relative merits of his different wins (and losses) in his running career, and I was struck by just how similar his belief system is to mine, in that for him one of the key, defining moments of his career was not in winning, but in losing. Not the act of losing itself – which is always painful and not something you should ever seek or set out to do – but in the thinking and analysis that came after the defeat; in the realisation that in order to make the next step, to become the best in the world, there was more to do, more work required. If you are brave enough and far-sighted enough to nurture this type of honesty just when your self-defence mechanisms and blame reactions are at their peak, then there is real value there. The defeat is a catalyst that creates new understandings and insights into what is good, what needs to change and what needs to be got rid of in order to get to the next level. It took Seb Coe a good deal of self-interrogation and introspection to learn his lessons, and when he did, he went on to become one of the most formidable middle-distance runners the world has ever produced. The most insightful thing that he said is, on the face of it, completely obvious, but it resonated with me. He said that when you lose, sometimes it is simply because you're not good enough. Harnessing that understanding and turning it into a basis for development and improvement made all the difference to Lord Coe. It can for you, too. Another example of fear being harnessed for success is in a TV programme in the UK called *The Secret Millionaire*. The premise of the programme is a great one – financially successful people get dropped into deprived, poor areas of the country, where they spend a week under cover. They have to live on the bread-line, often in poor housing like everyone else around them, with very little money. They volunteer at charities, help out at youth clubs and day-care centres, and then at the end of the programme they reveal their true identity and give much-needed donations to certain people they have come to know. It is a great show for lots of reasons – not least of which because it is positively intentioned and reveals the strength and fortitude of those in need – but the facet of the show that strikes me most is just how often the secret millionaire has made a success out of their life despite tough and difficult upbringings themselves. Very few of them seem to have been born into wealth; they have fought and struggled and worked bloody hard to achieve. And almost to a man and woman, they share a real tangible fear of failure. They are determined to change their circumstance, they have known and endured hardship and they are absolutely driven not to be in the same situation ever again.

As you get more successful, you should continue to harness that fear of failure. Why? Because it is when you are a winner that fear can have the most profound positive effect. Imagine two changing rooms. In one, the captain of the side is urging his team to achieve something never before achieved – to beat the All Blacks. Under all of the hype and self-belief, there must be a bit of him that thinks, 'We might beat the All Blacks this weekend, but if we lose we are just one of the hundreds of other teams who have failed before us, no great shakes.' Sitting in the changing room next door however, there is a team that is thinking, 'I will *not* be in the first All Black team that ever loses to Ireland, or Scotland (or whoever). It just isn't going to happen.' That gives depth, desperation and commitment. Imagine being the first team to lose to Ireland in a hundred years. Heaven forbid. So you can imagine the captain's talk before the game. Fear drives you on and pushes you further. Once the spell is broken though, it is broken forever.

As my career progressed, I became increasingly driven by the fear of failure. I became increasingly aware that the reason – bad selections, bad luck, bad play – doesn't really matter if you lose. It says 'lost' next to the fixture in the history books, and my name is on that team sheet. I used that fear increasingly in my playing career, and I harnessed it consciously and continuously to drive myself on.

I was recently called by a journalist looking to get some comments and thoughts on the film *Invictus*, which focuses on events surrounding the Rugby World Cup in 1995 when we lost to South Africa – Mandela's World Cup. The journalist asked me if I had, in some way, reconciled myself to the fact that looking back it was a good thing for South Africa to win. It was a short interview. Anyone (although you've probably guessed he was an Englishman!) who suggests that losing doesn't matter hasn't really understood the Kiwi psyche, and certainly not the All Black psyche. Losing is a dreadful thing, period. It certainly isn't a cause for celebration.

Last year I watched the post-match interviews after Wales had lost to world champions South Africa at the Millennium stadium, and thought that what was said illustrated my point perfectly. One of the players – who had had a good game but should remain nameless – was talking about how good it was to have come so close to the World Champions and to have given them such a good game. I was sitting there watching, thinking, *Yeah, but you lost*. It didn't seem to me that the Welsh player had the right mental attitude. He wasn't afraid of losing, he almost seemed to accept it as an inevitability. If all the players felt that way, and so conversely none of them deep down, inside, really feared failure, it does make me wonder about the likelihood of them winning. To harness the fear of failure you have to really fear failure itself first. If you don't, then you can

Aim to win. If you do win, park it quickly. If you don't, use the failure. Take a positive out of it wherever you can. Reframe it not as a failure, but as feedback, as a necessary part of the process of winning.

have a lovely afternoon and be runner-up in a two-horse race. Not for me.

A FINAL THOUGHT ON EMBRACING THE FEAR OF FAILURE

Be careful that you don't end up believing that it is the taking part that counts. It isn't. It is the winning that counts . . . and if you are frightened of not winning, *and* can use that fear to spur you on, you have an edge. Fear of failure has been a massive driver in my career and my pursuance of being the best that I can be. Failure happens. Fact. That is the same for everyone, everywhere – I defy you to find anyone who has not at some point experienced failure. The trick is in how you handle it, and how you deal with it.

On a collective level, that World Cup semi-final defeat by Australia in Ireland signalled the end of that All Black team. It was a sad time – we had such talent but we fell apart. We arrived home with our tails between our legs. It wasn't long before the disappointment of the World Cup failure morphed into anger. Changes were needed and Grizz Wylie, our coach, was given his marching orders. On a personal level, I wondered whether that might be it for me. I was acutely aware of my own vulnerability, and I was half expecting to be cut from the team. When I heard that the new coach was to be Laurie Mains, I wasn't comforted. He was a tough man, a traditionalist, and a very different character to those with whom I had got on well in my playing career. When Laurie joined the set-up in 1992, I knew that my international career hung in the balance, and that fear of failing – of ending my All Black career in this ignominious manner – meant that I had to have a plan. I figured the best one was to keep my head down, work my bloody socks off and do whatever I needed to do to keep my berth. Basically that involved staying out of trouble and avoiding the limelight.

Nice plan. But, as it turned out, not a chance . . .

SIX

LEARNING FROM TRADITION

ONE OF THE MOST ROMANTIC stories I have heard about the All Black jersey concerns the silver fern emblem – the national symbol of New Zealand – that adorns the breast. Legend has it that the silver fern was abundant in the natural New Zealand vegetation, and Maori warriors, returning through the night to their families and tribes after war or hunting, would turn the silver ferns to catch the moonlight and so illuminate their path home. There may not be an ounce of truth in it, but it captures a little of the magic that is contained within the symbol, and, by association, the jersey. The New Zealand rugby jersey is itself enshrouded with folklore and legend, steeped in history and tradition. And perhaps it was because of this that when I was growing up, I would never have worn an All Black jersey out in public. I'd run around in the backyard all day in an All Black jersey, but out on the street? No way. Unless you were an All Black you would never dare to put the jersey on in public. Then again, even if you *were* an All Black, heaven forbid you'd actually have the arrogance to march down the street with your bloody jersey on! In those days it was all very different, but while the power and the currency of the actual physical jersey might have been eroded in recent times with the exponential growth of the replica jersey market, the All Black jersey itself remains potent. Every nation has a symbol that represents their country – the English have their rose, the Scots their thistle and the South Africans their springbok. For us Kiwis, the silver fern represents a deep and emotional attachment to our country and our rugby; it is a symbol that speaks of pride, winning and excellence. An Adidas advert summed it up brilliantly when it said of the All Black jersey 'the legacy is more intimidating than any opposition'.

As the players wearing that jersey in the 1991 loss to Australia, we had fallen short of those expectations and so individually and collectively we were both culpable . . . and vulnerable. When Laurie Mains arrived as the incoming coach, there was a strong sense that a new broom was sweeping through the All Blacks. One of the first things Laurie did when he arrived was to axe Gary Whetton as captain. He chopped him not only from the captaincy, but also from the side and the squad – Gary wasn't even given a trial. He was gone.

In what was to be the centenary season for the All Blacks (and so a season where the captain would be thrust into the limelight even more than usual), it was pretty clear that Mains already knew who his skipper was going to be when he arrived. Laurie had made Mike Brewer – a hugely talented back row player – his captain once already, when he was coach of Otago in 1985, and so he was generally recognised as the heir apparent when Gary Whetton was

Dad (left) during his Wainui Surf Lifesaving days.

Dad and his Gisborne Boys High 1st XV team-mates, 1948.

LEFT: *Being put to good use as a youngun.*

BELOW: *Receiving the Secondary School Player of the Year Award from Sir Wilson Whineray.*

LEFT: *I could do more than rugby! Here I am pre-game, all dressed as captain of the Sacred Heart College 1st XI cricket team.*

ABOVE: *With the guys from the Auckland University team, having won the Gallagher Shield.*

BELOW: *With the Monday night touch team.*

ABOVE: *(left) Andy Haden.* SPORTING CONTACTS LTD; *(right) Francois Pienaar.* PHOTOSPORT

BELOW: *With John Hart.* PHOTOSPORT

ABOVE: *Laurie Mains.* PHOTOSPORT

BELOW: *At the 2008 Laureus World Sports Awards, with Steve Waugh (left) and Shane Warne.*

ABOVE: *With Gareth Edwards and Kenny Dalglish, 2008.*

BELOW: *About to present the Fitzpatrick/Kirkpatrick Cup, contested annually between Sacred Heart and Kings College.*

ABOVE: *Our girls: Eva (left) and Grace.*

LEFT: *With my wife, Bronwyn.*

BELOW: *Co-author and friend Andy FitzGerald, with his son Archie.*

so unceremoniously shown the door. Most people agreed that Brewer was a good choice.

I was a little more lucky than Gary, but only just. I got a phone call where Laurie asked me, 'Sean, do you want to be an All Black again?' I replied, 'Yes Laurie, I'd love to be an All Black again.' He said, 'Well, you're probably not going to be. One, you're too slow. Two, you're too fat. Three, you're bloody arrogant, and four [which hurt me most of all] you've lost the respect for the All Black jersey. If you can show me in six weeks that you've changed, I'll give you an opportunity in the All Black trial.'

Laurie had made the situation pretty simple for me. The new coach was a man with whom I didn't share a great rapport. He'd got his captain pretty much inked in and he was looking around to make other changes and construct a new side, to resurrect All Black fortunes by bringing in new blood, different players. My only priority at this stage was to make sure that I kept hold of the jersey, and that I didn't end my All Black career as a victim of the poor performance of recent matches, and the wholesale changing of the guard going on at the top. I focused all my efforts in making sure that during the trial games Laurie held, I put myself about as much as possible. I revved myself up, played hard and gave every ounce of energy I had. I played well enough to be selected as captain of the 'Possibles' side against the 'Probables' and it was looking like (although still by no means certain) that I was at least in with a shout.

Then, in the final trial game – basically a rubber-stamping of the decisions that Laurie had already made – Mike Brewer got injured. He was clearly going to be out for a few games at least. From nowhere, the whole momentum that was being generated under Laurie was under threat, and with his first choice captain now unavailable for what was to be a big year, he was going to have to go to plan B. We sat and waited in the dressing room afterwards for what seemed like an age while the selectors discussed and argued about exactly what – or who – that Plan B was going to be.

I vividly remember sitting in that changing room and looking at the players around me, and slowly it dawned on me that I was probably one of the names being considered. A knot started forming in the pit of my stomach. I was nervous enough about retaining my place, but suddenly, with Mike Brewer on the treatment table and out of contention, there was a chance that I was in the running for the ultimate job in world rugby. *Bloody hell*, I thought. I got my first start as an All Black because of someone else's misfortune . . . I played in the World Cup side because of someone else's misfortune . . . was I about to have the same thing happen to me again?

I was. Laurie – I suspect with some misgivings – named me as captain of the New Zealand All Blacks in the centenary year and there couldn't have been a man more proud – or more nervous – than me in the whole of the country that day. An ex-Prime Minister of New Zealand, Jim Bolger, is supposed to have once said, 'When the All Blacks win, I'd love to be their captain. When they lose, I'm glad I'm only the Prime Minister.' I think that is a great quote, and it goes some way to illustrating the importance of the role of the All Blacks captain. It is not a position to be taken on lightly, it comes to only a few men, and for me it is the greatest honour in rugby that I can imagine.

But it is also *pressure*. People have a huge expectation and that is channelled into the captain, and through the captain. If the team isn't playing well, he gets it in the neck. But more than the expectation of the New Zealand public, I think the captain of the All Blacks understands – or should understand – the huge responsibility to every All Black

Fact is, if you're made captain, you are captain. No sense debating endlessly about whether you're ready for it, or what skills you possess or lack; you have to knuckle down and *be* the captain. Be the leader.

that has gone before him, to everyone that has ever pulled the jersey on, and to every captain that has led the New Zealand national side out since the start of the great adventure over one hundred years ago. In other words, he has to acknowledge that the tradition that comes with the territory is an important element of the role – it has to be maintained, developed and learned from.

If I am completely honest, I was absolutely petrified by the whole prospect. My initial reaction was that I didn't want to be the captain at all. In fact, early on I got it into my head that I didn't know or understand enough about the role, and so in an effort to get my head around it, I got in touch with a number of past captains and asked them for advice; about what they'd learnt as captain and what they'd do again, and about what they'd do differently if they had their time again. It still sounds like a good idea even now as I write it, but I can specifically remember sitting down with Andy Dalton in his big office and he was looking at me as if I was mad. I said to him, 'Andy, I don't think I am prepared to be the All Black captain.' And he just kept on looking at me, not saying a word, but written all over his face was, 'What the f**k is this boy talking about?!' All he said to me was, 'Well, mate, you *are* the All Black captain, so you'd better get bloody used to it!' Maybe not the depth of analysis or insight I was looking for, but in fact what he said resonated with me years later. It isn't about learning and theory and taking tips and ideas off others – although all of that is of course important. Fact is, if you're made captain, you are captain. No sense debating endlessly about whether you're ready for it, or what skills you possess or lack; you have to knuckle down and *be* the captain. Be the leader.

Looking back on that time now, being thrown in at the deep end – unable to run away or hide – was a major turning point in my development. Fast forward through a blur of preparation for my first match as captain – against a World Fifteen to kick off the centenary celebrations – and at the final whistle, I am walking off the pitch with the unenviable record of captained one, lost one. I trudged inside, took an age to change, and reluctantly put my tie on with another sense of foreboding growing in the pit of my stomach. The speeches. I had just lost my first test as captain and I now had to give my first speech. The way that you have to do it as captain of the national side is pretty formulaic. You have to thank the other team, welcome the new caps (players who are representing the All Blacks for the first time), crack a couple of jokes and then get off. You have to be a good clear speaker and a fitting ambassador for the team, and in 'ordinary' circumstances I think I would have done all right. Except that on this occasion, as it was the centenary season, they'd only gone and invited every single living bloody All Black from the region, past and present, to the function. The room – or rather the marquee – had about a thousand people in it (okay, it may have only been a couple of hundred but it looked like and felt like a thousand!) and it was full to popping with legends and national heroes. Everywhere I looked, I saw the All Black tie, and generally it was tied around the neck of some huge, solid-looking, inscrutable farmer who was, I knew, waiting to see this Fitzy fella make his speech so they could get a measure of him as a worthy captain of their team . . . it was a room stuffed full of legend, of tradition – and I was the main act.

I ummed and I mumbled. I faltered through my opening bit. I was dry-mouthed, I was very nervous, and my delivery was just not good enough – looking back now, it was dreadful. When it came to the part of the speech where I was supposed to congratulate the new caps, the wheels came off good and proper. The first cap is of course a

Learning from tradition is about connecting past, present and future together. It recognises that just because something is new and shiny doesn't mean it is right, or better than what has gone before.

special moment and on this occasion it was made even more special for those players involved by me forgetting their names. Every one. We'd just lost to a World Fifteen – a team we should have put to bed a hundred times over – and now, a few short hours later, here I was, shame of shames, having the names of the new boys in the team shouted out to me by the audience. Not my greatest moment. I know I was new to the role, but I felt that I had let myself, my team and the All Black traditions of excellence down. If I was going to be an effective captain, if I was going to be as good a captain as I could be – and more importantly as good a captain as the All Blacks deserved – I had to get that sorted out, so I spent a good deal of time and effort in developing my public speaking, taking coaching and training lessons and working out how best to speak effectively in public. It was hard work, and initially it didn't come naturally to me, but with time and attention and practice, I got the hang of it; I even started to enjoy it. You can't get me off the bloody stage now!

Aside from the speeches, a key part of my role as captain of the All Blacks was, along with the coach and the management team, to look around the team and the group of players and continually be asking myself, 'How can this team become the best that it can be?' After a lot of discussion with Laurie and the more senior players, it became evident to me that one of the critical elements missing in the changing room was the understanding of, and respect for, the history and tradition of the All Blacks. This wasn't a deliberate thing, as all New Zealanders, players included, had an innate sense of how special the All Blacks are; but somehow over recent years it had been pushed a little bit into the background. In the drive towards ever better performance, we had begun to focus so much on what we were trying to do that perhaps we'd lost sight of *who we were*, of where we had come from, and of the duty and responsibility that rested on our shoulders. We had a history and a tradition that was second to none in world rugby, but we weren't leveraging it. That had to change.

The traditions of the All Black family had to be celebrated and put back to the very centre of who we were and what we were about. Keeping the traditions of the team alive and preserving them amidst all the changes that the game and the team had seen – and will continue to see – is vital. The traditions that have been handed down from year to year and team to team are in fact the glue that binds together every All Black across the years. It is tradition that makes it so much more than just a black jersey. Some of the traditions were just impromptu repetitions that were passed from team to team. The 'back of the bus' conversations mentioned earlier were a good example of that. Even here, they've definitely suffered as players use iPods and Walkmans and zone out on the way to games, and teams get flown everywhere rather than spending hour after hour on the tour bus. Perhaps there are 'back of the Jumbo' chats now. Another example was the tradition we had when we toured in the UK and crossed the Severn Bridge to go into Wales, when we would all stand up and shout at the top of our voices, 'We Never Lose In Wales!' Okay, so in terms of pomp and circumstance it might not be right up there with the Queen's Coronation, but when we did it we felt the echo of generations of All Blacks who we knew had done exactly the same thing, at exactly the same moment. It was an All Black tradition.

Of course, some All Black traditions are much more substantial than just tour bus antics. The Maori haka is one such example. A central tradition both of Maori and (more recently, in the last century or so) All Black culture, it is probably the single strongest association with New Zealand rugby. Before every match, the team now perform the haka. With its origins shaped over thousands of years, a Maori tribe's ability in the haka was a matter of supreme social importance. The dance was, and remains, a custom within Polynesian culture through which a tribe's status can rise or fall. Portraying their deeds and valour, their status and bravery, and displaying protest or defiance, every line and every movement has deep significance.

The Originals took the haka with them on their first overseas tour, and it fast became the pre-match party piece performed by the exotic touring side. In fact it was never performed at home, only ever on tour, right up until 1987 at the Rugby World Cup. Because the All Blacks would, in effect, be touring New Zealand, we decided to use it as part of our pre-match preparations. We did so, and before very long performing the haka before every match was the norm. Our captain in 1987 was a guy called Wayne 'Buck' Shelford – a huge man in every sense and the absolute epitome of an All Black. Big, hard, committed, ruthless and brave, he was absolutely instrumental in lifting the profile of the haka both with the public, and with the team themselves.

An aside, for those of you who are interested in looking at what a haka is, and how to react to it, go to YouTube and type in 'Ireland, Willie Anderson, haka' – and have a look at a big, mad Irishman coming up against Buck Shelford as the All Black captain led the haka at Lansdowne Road, the Irish rugby ground. Priceless. Another interesting one is the Tana Umaga-led haka that was first performed against South Africa when he was captain. A truly awesome sight.

Of course there is plenty of opinion in world rugby that the haka gives us an unfair advantage. Certainly we use it as best we can to impose ourselves on opponents and fans (and whole nations if necessary) but I make absolutely no apology for that. It is part of who we are, and what we do before kick off – as long as we are not rude or offensive to anyone – is our own business.

One small but important contribution to this focus on our rugby tradition, that took place shortly after my time as captain, was in putting together something that we called *The Little Black Book*. After the All Blacks had lost five games in a row in 1998 (and yes it still hurts even just putting that down on paper!), I got a call from a great friend of mine and fellow ex-All Black John Kirwan – JK to his mates. We were no longer playing for the team, but that didn't stop him from being pretty forthright with me. 'Fitzy,' he said, 'you haven't done your job. You've not inducted these All Blacks the way that we were inducted. They're losing games without giving the fight of their lives, they're taking their position for granted, and they don't respect the All Black jersey. You and I are going to write a book.' Well JK and I are a butcher and a builder by trade, so I put his ranting and raving down to a fierce patriotism and too much Coca-Cola, but sure enough, we got together with some other ex-All Blacks and we worked through – I hesitate to say it but I suppose I've avoided it for long enough in this chapter – the All Black *brand*. Because in effect that is what I now realise we were dealing with – it was a matter of brand. The signs and signals, the emotional attachments and reactions that surrounded the All Black brand needed to be polished and protected, noted and shared. At the time of course, I had no such highfalutin notions. All we knew was that with a disillusioned public and a run of poor recent results, we needed to protect the magic of the All Blacks. The answer to this lay in part through focusing in on our traditions and stories. As one older ex-player and All Black captain bluntly explained to me when we were researching *The Little Black Book*, 'In my day we didn't have to write this bloody stuff down!' He was right of course; and it

In the drive towards ever better performance, we had begun to focus so much on what we were trying to do that perhaps we'd lost sight of *who we were*, of where we had come from, and of the duty and responsibility that rested on our shoulders.

reminded me of the importance of formalising the tradition a little more than we had done.

BACKGROUND: SO WHAT WAS IN THE BOOK?

That you honour the All Black jersey first and foremost with honesty – that you have to be true to yourself and your team. That humility is a requirement of the job too – you can't ever think that you've made it. That respect is a foundation stone of the All Black tradition and that honouring history and achievement – and having reverence for that – is important. That loyalty to the jersey, the team and most of all to the belief that in the heat of battle, however hard and impossible it seems, never wavering and staying true to the commitment of winning is the All Black way. That you never take your jersey for granted. That you be humble. Once an All Black always an All Black, and that it is an honour, not a job. That the All Blacks are aiming to be *great* not good. That you turn up early, work harder than the next guy. That you fear failure. And that if you have to give feedback, do it to their face, not behind someone's back – belly not back.

The book was about setting down the All Black brand and providing a shared language, a system of meanings that everyone understood – a language and vocabulary and a set of beliefs that bound the group together.

And it's not a new idea. Look at any family. The stories about Uncle getting drunk and riding his bicycle into the ditch, or Grandma marching into the pub with a rolling pin to get Granddad home for Sunday lunch, or the distant aunt who kept 11 cats and could recite Shakespeare – the million and one stories that exist within families and across generations serve to bring everyone involved, directly or indirectly, together. These tales and stories become a shared set of memories and values that bind everyone involved together, and they become a compelling force. There is little so comforting and empowering as being with your tribe, laughing together, retelling tales and sharing understanding. Sharing and celebrating who you are and what you stand for is a basic human instinct.

AN IDEA TO TRY: FINDING YOUR OWN TRADITIONS

It is the tradition surrounding the All Blacks that creates such passion and belief in those who play in the black jersey. You can't be at your best until you are passionate about what you are doing. What are your passions, your traditions? Take some time to examine that question. Acknowledge the value that stories and traditions, rituals and symbols have. Seek them out. What are the rituals and symbols that have a positive part to play in your life and your world? If you can't find any, make some. It gives a whole new level of meaning and motivation to what you're doing.

Taking your position for granted is a dumb move. Thinking it will last for ever is even dumber.

Of course I'm not naïve enough to believe that every New Zealand rugby international had the same outlook as I have about the duty and responsibility that comes with being an All Black. I have certainly seen some players, even some All Blacks, who in my view abused their position and took what they could from as many people as they could. Being an All Black means everyone loves you, especially in New Zealand. I have seen that being taken advantage of – people doing deals and demanding freebies, acting like prima donnas and getting away with it because they were an All Black. I have seen huge arrogance, with players treating those around them dismissively. It was all *take, take, take*, but once they'd finished playing, no one wanted to know them. It struck me as immensely sad that while these guys were at the pinnacle of their sport and in such an honoured position, they didn't realise the duty and responsibility that came along with that – they took the short-term gains and were immeasurably poorer for it. Sad. Taking your position for granted is a dumb move. Thinking it will last for ever is even dumber. They didn't learn from tradition. They will not leave a legacy.

AN IDEA TO TRY: WHAT IS YOUR LEGACY?

I believe that nothing is more important than the legacy that you leave, and such a simple question – 'what is your legacy?' can, when you answer it, have a huge impact on clarifying those things that are important and those things that you want to focus on, that are important to you. By legacy I am not talking about the amount of money that you will leave, or whether you should build a hospital wing or an art gallery (but if you have the cash, do both). I mean more about how you want to be remembered. What will be the stories that are told about you? How will people reference you when you're gone – what values and attributes will people associate with you? It is a really useful and focusing exercise to spend some time sitting thinking about these questions and trying to write it all down. It does feel a little bit like writing your own obituary, but it is a powerful exercise to enable you to focus on those core values that are most important to you.

A FINAL THOUGHT ON LEARNING FROM TRADITION

You can't walk backwards into tomorrow. The world changes, things move on and to succeed you need to be agile, flexible and open to doing things differently. That said, however, I am absolutely certain that having been involved in the All Blacks for so long, tradition can teach us many things. Since the All Blacks first got together to play rugby and represent a nation, every player and coach involved has been looking to learn and improve on what has been before. Anything that is counter-productive, or negative or useless is discarded, thrown out. Those traditions within the All Blacks that have remained then, whether they be songs or sayings, processes or protocol, serve to connect us back through all the players that have shared it with us, all the way back to James Allan (All Black Number 1) in 1884.

Learning from tradition is about connecting past, present and future together. It recognises that just because something is new and shiny doesn't mean it is right, or better than what has gone before. I absolutely believe that we all need to think carefully about where and how we can learn from the past, from tradition, in order to be sure that we don't lose touch with who we are and where we have come from – and in the process lose sight of what is important as we journey on.

SEVEN

LEADING FROM THE FRONT

I WANT TO START THIS CHAPTER about leading from the front by explaining a little bit about the loss that I perhaps felt the most keenly, against the Springboks in the 1995 Rugby World Cup final. We went to the World Cup in South Africa that year with the wind in our sails and a lot of self-belief. We believed that we were capable of playing the sort of irresistible, quick rugby that had eluded us the previous year, and as the pool games progressed, we began to gain momentum through the competition. As captain I made sure that I was front and centre in terms of my approach and attitude. I was absolutely committed, I was confident without being arrogant, and I spent every minute of every waking hour focusing in on the task in hand. As a team, we approached the final stages with intense determination.

Elsewhere, though, we could also see South Africa doing the same thing . . . but in their case the momentum wasn't just confined to the players on the pitch. As they progressed through the competition, the Springboks seemed to awaken the whole South African nation. Nelson Mandela had recognised the importance of the rugby team to the white South African population and, insightful as ever, he had also realised the value of embracing their quest instead of marginalising it in those fragile days when distrust and fear were prevalent between the black and white citizens he was leading. He turned the South African World Cup campaign into a crusade for the Rainbow nation. The team became an expression of the unity of the country, and black and white South Africans rallied to their cause.

Which, as it turned out, was a real bugger for us.

We lost in the final to a South African team that I believed – still believe – we should have beaten, and as our team's leader I found that hard to bear. I am still upset that we lost. I can't blank it out completely though. Not only did some fella make a film about it (and I understand Jack Nicholson would have *loved* to play me in the film but just couldn't make his schedule work), a movie which I have never – and will never – see, but I can also still vividly recall whole phases of the match as if it was last week. But most of all perhaps, I remember having to make the losing captain's speech at the do in the evening. Even as I stood up, I was seriously contemplating retirement. It had been a hard and brutal blow to lose in the manner we did to the team we did, and a part of me just wanted to draw a line and move on – giving up international rugby was a clear-cut way of doing that. That indecision and that blackness of spirit that enshrouded me on that evening was a career-low moment for me.

Leading from the front distils
down into a simple truth
against which you should
measure yourself and judge
your own performance.
Did you do your best?

AN IDEA TO TRY: A SIMPLE TRUTH

To lead from the front honestly and with real endeavour doesn't mean that you are going to succeed all the time. I have been in a number of situations where we fell short, just like in the World Cup of 1995, but whatever the outcome, leading from the front distils down into a simple truth against which you should measure yourself and judge your own performance. Did you do your best? Of course the urge and desire to win is all important, but to get there you have to be self-critical and honest, and sometimes you just fall short. If, though, in the midst of defeat and disappointment, you can put your hand on your heart and say that you did your best, all the time, every time, then however big the disappointment, you can still sleep at night. It may be small comfort, but it is a comfort, and it is important.

Of course, I was clear about the need to maintain some perspective on matters . . . I had lost a rugby game, not my liberty. The definitive example of 'leading from the front' is Nelson Mandela. I first met him in 1992 when we had a short tour of South Africa – the first since the fall of Apartheid – which culminated in us beating them in the single test match. Nelson Mandela was at a lot of the games we played; we shook hands and exchanged a few pleasantries. I met Mr Mandela again during the South African World Cup campaign. As I shook his hand just before the final, I remember thinking that I had missed a trick – I should have got him to wear an All Black jersey for the occasion. In 2000 our paths crossed once more, through my involvement in the Laureus Sport For Good Foundation. I have therefore had the privilege to shake hands, talk to, and spend time with a man who has led a nation from the front, away from violence and retribution and towards conciliation and celebration in a way that has been as inspiring as it has been humbling.

BACKGROUND: WHAT IS LAUREUS?

The Laureus Sport For Good Foundation is the brainchild of Johann Rupert, the billionaire South African businessman who owns the luxury goods group Richemont. Mr Rupert has a passion for business and has presided over the development of a phenomenal stable of international luxury brands – Dunhill, Cartier, Montblanc, Piaget, Net-a-Porter, Van Cleef and Arpels – the list goes on and on. Mr Rupert's other passion is sport. He understands that it can do a huge amount of good in the world, and so through Laureus he has leveraged his wealth to harness this potential. The very best individuals (and teams) from the world of sport are invited to join the Academy. People like Boris Becker, Ed Moses, Nadia Comaneci, Sir Bobby Charlton, Steve Waugh, Gary Player, Ian Botham; it's quite a list. We all get treated royally at an annual awards night, but more importantly we are also given the platform to show that sport can be used for good. Each of us gets involved in supporting sports initiatives around the world that are changing peoples lives for the better, sometimes in difficult conditions and tough places. It is a charity that I think leads from the front in terms of how it leverages the power of sport for good. It is great to be involved.

My dark days passed very quickly. I had no time to mope about, because with the ending of the World Cup, a new competition began – for the very future of rugby. With this came one of my greatest leadership challenges. The game had already begun to turn professional, but after 1995's Rugby World Cup, the pace quickened considerably. Two very different and conflicting paths emerged, and increasingly it became clear that it was the players, and not the managers or administrators, who were going to have the final say. Whoever had the players under their control had the game of rugby under their control, and with the largely untapped potential of the sport still to be realised around the world, that was a prize worth chasing.

On the one hand, players had the option of being paid within the current structure and format of the game – essentially a maintenance of the status quo, but with money. This approach was being put together by Rupert Murdoch, who was negotiating with the unions from each country (in other words the administrators and managers of the game) and was confident of closing the deal.

In the other corner though, there was a deal being put together by Kerry Packer, an Australian multi-millionaire who wanted to fundamentally change how the game was structured; his plan was to sign up all the international players from every country and put franchise teams together, where players would form completely new teams based in different cities around the world and be paid huge

Authenticity is about showing your strengths and also the things you're not so good at. You don't have to be perfect in everything and followers want a 'real' leader, someone who is comfortable to show both strengths and weaknesses.

amounts of money to play, with finance generated from TV deals and advertising.

Throughout 1995, Murdoch had been working hard and had signed all the unions to his plan without us players even knowing. It was announced on the Friday of the World Cup final week as a great deal that would take rugby forward into the professional era. In the meantime however, Packer's boys were signing all the players! He'd got most of the Australians, as well as some of the South Africans, and he was flashing the cash and in so doing, fast gaining momentum and credibility. He approached us All Blacks on the Sunday after the World Cup final. I'd been out for a game of golf and when I got back one of the team came to tell me that Packer's boys were here and that he'd just had a conversation with them. We met them as a squad – all 30 players, without the coaches, to hear what he had to say. I said from the very beginning that I was happy to go down this road, support it and front it up on behalf of the Kiwi players, *but* . . . there was a but. That was that we would all have to go down the road together. If we started splitting, we were lost and it was not going to happen. We agreed – it was everyone in or no deal. Packer was offering an incredible amount of money a year, but the New Zealand Rugby Union came to us and said that Murdoch would match it, so it was clear that the decision was not primarily a monetary one. There were two offers on the table, two identical amounts of money there for the players – but the big decision was which one would fly, and which one would be best for New Zealand rugby.

Publicly there was a God Almighty row. The whole country seemed to turn against us for considering the Packer option, and it was a difficult few weeks, for sure. For us players, the global phone lines were white-hot, with the captains of all the teams calling each other to discuss the issue. It was a mad time and brought a whole new set of questions to worry about as the All Black captain. There seemed to be a lot of whispered agreements and shaking hands in dark corners, and although as a squad we believed the Packer deal was the right option, we were clear that it would only work if every single international team and all the key players – particularly the World Champions South Africa – signed up. The simple fact of the matter was that if the South Africans weren't in this new global game that Packer was proposing, it wouldn't work.

In the end, the decision was made for us. The South African captain, Francois Pienaar, and some of their other key players pulled out of the Packer proposal at the very last second and went with Murdoch. That one withdrawal, because it was from such a high-profile player, snowballed and soon the whole South African team fell over. Our guys started jumping ship as a result and, put simply, that was the end of that. We had said all along that it was everyone or no one, so when I was asked what I wanted to do by the chairman of New Zealand rugby, I pulled out too. The Packer deal never happened, the unions kept control of the players, and the game survived pretty much in the same form as it had always been.

Perhaps the most important outcome of the whole affair was that players, management, sponsors and administrators alike were all presented with the crystal-clear fact that the players were increasingly important to the future of the game; it was no longer just in the hands of the law-makers or the anonymous committee men. Players had to be considered more, respected more, and given more. It was a wake-up call that was too long in the coming, but finally it was being heard.

Of course, I've since spoken to Francois about the whole Packer situation, and it is clear that they were put in a difficult position; but when they broke the deal, quite a few players from other countries thought they were wrong, and blamed them for making a bad decision. I think Francois is still convinced that it was me who got him carried off on a stretcher in Cape Town when we played there later in 1996, as payback for him not getting on board with the Packer thing, but it really didn't happen like that. Francois and I are good mates now, I see him quite a bit on the circuit . . . but I do know that even to this day there is still bitterness among some players who blame the South Africans for scuppering their best shot at a load of cash and a globally exciting circus of rugby.

For my part, I have no issues about either how it went, or how it might have gone. I know that some people called us mercenaries at the time, but the truth is that I was totally up front and honest with everyone. I had nothing to hide and I have no misgivings about what happened or how I – or my team – conducted themselves. It was certainly a whole conversation about the game that needed to be had, and I was absolutely up for leading from the front – at least for the All Blacks – while we had it.

In my life after rugby, one of the most asked questions that people come to me with is about my leadership – what was my leadership style? I know that there are a million and one different theories and schools of thought about leadership. To be honest, some of the stuff I read makes me laugh – it is so intricate and theoretical that I couldn't even bloody understand it, let alone put it into action when the fur was flying and some big Celt was trying to rip my head off – but I have found a couple of useful ideas that I think describe it well.

There are two London Business School professors called Rob Goffee and Gareth Jones who defined leadership as 'exciting others to higher performance'. I like that – it is nice and simple and it gives the sense of the fact that you are leading from the front to get a result, to get improved performance from your team. If not, why bother being there? They go on to say that the people following the leader perform best if four things are present, and again I think they make good sense and describe leadership in a way that I understand and can recognise.

Firstly, they say that all the team are looking for community, and I recognise that – it is the idea of the band of brothers, the 'we happy few' concept where the team gives the individual a sense of belonging and identity.

Secondly, they are looking for authenticity in their leader, in that he or she has to have a genuine and true set of beliefs and principles that guide them, not just an approach that is PR-driven or insincere. Moreover, authenticity is about showing your strengths and also the things you're not so good at. You don't have to be perfect in everything and followers want a 'real' leader, someone who is comfortable to show both strengths and weaknesses.

Thirdly, the leader also has to demonstrate significance – they can't just be there because of their status; they have to add value . . . *and* each individual member of the team needs to know that their contribution is seen as significant too.

Finally, these guys say that team members want excitement from their leader – a sense of mission and purpose that gets the old heart fluttering and sets sinew, mind and muscle alight.

As well as talking to my team and keeping them focused on the task in hand, I would talk to referees, linesmen, the opposition, my opposite number – I made sure that I got out in front and made my presence felt.

AN IDEA TO TRY: NOW VERSUS NEXT WEEK . . .

Leading from the front means doing it now. Do it better today and tomorrow, not next week. When you close this book after you finish reading it, commit to a change. It only needs to be one thing. It doesn't need to change the world. But it needs to be something that, in changing, will improve you and your situation. Success is all about modest improvements consistently done. Start today. Leave NOTHING on the table. Put your heart and soul into it. Wherever you are and however far away your goal sounds at the moment, you can get closer to it by starting the process. Have the balls to change. Start doing shit. Accept and understand that sacrifice is key. Make the sacrifices willingly, and focus on making them worthwhile. Start today.

We were certainly on a mission after losing the World Cup. As the leader of that losing team, I had taken the decision to continue, and it wasn't long before I felt re-energised. I had re-found my mojo and was gunning for excellence, determined to use that defeat as a spur. We were certainly in the right year – we had a Tri-Nations tournament (a tough three-way competition between New Zealand, South Africa and Australia where you play each side both home and away) followed by a test series in South Africa. That represented a huge challenge and motivation for us because unbelievably the All Blacks had never, in their long and illustrious history, won a test series in South Africa. It was a Holy Grail for us Kiwis, and to my mind it was definitely possible.

Playing against the Boks in Christchurch in the Tri-Nations tournament, a bloke called John Allen headbutted me as we settled in to the first scrum. It became a bit of a talking point afterwards, but it also provided us with a focus for our discussions about how to take the Springboks in their own backyard when we toured there a few weeks later. Mr Allen helped us to clear our minds for the South Africa expedition, and we went there the next month with one central strategy – to dominate them in the scrum. I believed that he had shown us with his headbutt that he was edgy, nervous . . . and generally when players are like that it is because they don't know if they measure up. I took that as a gift from the Boks – our approach was going to be in their face, right up the middle, full on and brutal.

Now it may not have been the most intellectual of approaches but it was a good simple plan, it played to our strengths, and the squad got behind it. And for me, the real beauty of the plan was that I was going to be right in the middle of it all. The leader. I had the opportunity, with the approach we were going to take, to lead from the front. Ah, happy days! There are, of course, lots of situations where as a leader you have to lead from the front metaphorically – morally perhaps, or in terms of hours worked, or maybe speed of service – whatever it is, it can sometimes be a lot less tangible to both the leader and the team. But for me, in that tour and those matches I had the perfect opportunity to literally, *physically* lead from the front. To be able to stand as captain in front of my national team, ready to go to war, staring down big, ugly, dribbling Afrikaaners on the other side of the halfway line was just about as good as it gets, I reckon. I count myself as one of the luckiest men alive to have had that privilege. The team talks, the haka, the set-piece moves and the tactical decisions were all part of my job of course, but primary objective number one was to be in *every* fight and brawl around the park; to be first in and last out of close quarter battles; to work like a dog for 80 minutes; to show no fear and to give no quarter; *to lead from the front*. It was the best time I've ever had on a rugby pitch. We went on to win the series.

At this stage in my career, being captain was becoming second nature. It brought with it a lot of pressure that came in a number of different forms, but I knew what I was; I was the CEO of the All Blacks and everything I said or did – or didn't say or didn't do – would have an impact. As the leader of the All Blacks I couldn't *not* communicate either on or off the pitch. During that 80 minutes there was the personal pressure of knowing that you had to perform, and do so in such a way that underlined your position and authority – and not just with the players but with the press and the general public too. In a perverse way I enjoyed that pressure. I certainly enjoyed a certain notoriety with regard to how I played and I knew that very often I was going to be a marked man. And I thought, *Well, so be it!* My view was that you can mark me all you like, but at some stage during this match you are going to have to go toe-to-toe with me – and when that happens, I will be ready, and I will give as good – or better – than I get. I made sure that I was at the centre of everything. As well as talking to my team and keeping them focused on the task in hand, I would talk to referees, linesmen, the opposition, my opposite number – whoever was around, I made sure that I got out in front and made my presence felt. I made sure that I was a physical and verbal presence on the field of play, and although it wasn't always a conscious decision – I think I just like to be in the middle of things – it paid real dividends. By helping the referee whenever they needed a wee bit of advice, or pointing out specific deficiencies (technical, personal or genetic, I didn't mind) in my opposite number, I believe that I was leading from the front, and showing my team that I was in charge. I know that this approach caused a degree of irritation in a few people that I played against but I'm not sorry for that. I played to win, and if I developed a reputation that helped us to achieve that, then it was well worth doing.

AN IDEA TO TRY: FINDING THE BALANCE

The balancing of pride and humility is a tough one to get right, but make sure that however good you get, whatever successes you achieve, you 'leave it on the field'. Pride and sunglasses come before a fall, and just when you think you're at your untouchable best, fate will conspire to knock you back down. Keep at the very heart of who you are and what you do the fact that, in an uncertain world, the one thing that you can affect is your own performance. Your performance is infectious and what you project out to other people – the way that you approach the challenges in front of you – will be how they begin to act, and behave. Be proud, of course, and focused, and driven. But don't become arrogant.

In the intense environment of a fast-moving game of international rugby, you also have to be able to dissociate from the game you are playing at a personal level, and objectively evaluate and make decisions almost continuously. I am glad to say that this came naturally to me.

You can't always choose
what you do, but you
absolutely can choose
the attitude that you
bring to it.

I was a keen student of the game, and playing in the front row I was able to get a good feel for the ebb and flow from the coalface. It was often clear to me that the impact of my decisions would have an effect on the outcome of the game, and I really enjoyed that.

To lead effectively you have to keep your players focused and on plan. That means getting to know your team, and the individuals within it, and knowing how to press the different buttons for the different personalities. Some players need cajoling, some bullying, and some need time, attention and gentle persuasion. The important thing is to have fixed in your mind the outcome that you want, not the way that you are going to get there. If one approach doesn't work, use another one, but all the time you have to be listening, watching and understanding what is making the different members of your team tick.

You also hold ultimate responsibility for the culture within the team. Very often a team will take on the traits and characteristics of its leader, and in my case that wouldn't always have been a good thing! I have Laurie Mains to thank for teaching me that lesson. One evening, on tour in my early days as captain, I was just cracking a couple of beers with one or two of the boys in the team room, while the rest of the squad were off elsewhere, when Laurie came in. To his absolute credit Laurie made us put the beer back and he told us in no uncertain terms that there were to be no cliques, no drinking in small groups – we would wait for the whole team or we wouldn't drink at all. I don't think Laurie trusted me as captain at this stage, but I thought long and hard about the incident that night, and I respected Laurie for that and for many other instances when he demonstrated his commitment to the cause and his clarity of thinking on the important ingredients of leadership. Leading from the front isn't a part-time role that you can pick up and set down as and when it suits. You have to do it *all the time* and *every time*.

A consistent, considered approach engenders loyalty . . . and loyalty to the team, within a team, and from the team are critical factors of success. Loyalty manifests itself in many different ways – in the decisions that are made, the way people work together, the team spirit that exists. It manifests itself in a hundred tiny ways too – the guy who didn't make the starting line-up remaining utterly committed to the cause; the time, care and attention to detail that the coaches put in to preparing a session; loyalty to the team – and the cause – is a precious commodity.

It is linked too to 'discretionary effort', a phrase and an idea which I like. This is defined as 'the difference that makes the difference' – in other words those things over and above what could be reasonably expected of you, that you do anyway because they contribute to the wider enterprise. Good teams don't become great just because people do their jobs well. They become great because every last person in the team is continually looking for ways to put more effort in; they take responsibility for the team as a whole and every minute of every day is spent finding ways to put more in. And leading from the front means putting more effort in than anybody. Be the last guy off the training pitch, or the guy who has prepared more than anyone else for the meeting, or the person who will stay late to finish a project. Be the first one out to the pitch, or be early, be prepared, be ready well before you're due to start your day's work. You can't always choose what you do, but you absolutely can choose the attitude that you bring to it.

The one thing that you can affect
is your own performance. Your
performance is infectious and what
you project out to other people
– the way that you approach the
challenges in front of you – will be
how they begin to act, and behave.

A FINAL THOUGHT ON LEADING FROM THE FRONT

The truth is that rugby is a very simple game. There are a number of basics that you have to nail in order to win: keeping possession, maintaining momentum and 'going forward', simple passing, kicking and tackling – these are the foundations upon which success is built. It is the same story for leadership and leading from the front: the basic rules of life apply. These rules have been given to me by my parents, my family and the society that I grew up in (because I do think we Kiwis have an approach to life that works!). These basic rules are the simple things like being honest with yourself and others, appreciation and respect, and having clear principles and values that guide you. You have got to nail those, appreciate those, believe in those if you're going to get on. Doing the basics well matters, whoever you are, and whatever you do. Make no mistake, if you are leading from the front, everybody is watching – so take pride, and do it right.

EIGHT

DRIVING CHANGE

THE LAST TOUR OF THE UK was a painful one for me. In physical terms, with a knee that was increasingly misbehaving and giving way on me, I had consistently high and sustained aggravation and discomfort as I basically ignored it and carried on playing. Psychologically too, as it stubbornly refused to fix, a sense of fore-boding and worry was developing – I was beginning to feel that this was possibly the end of my career. It was a difficult time and I became preoccupied. I tightened up both on and off the pitch as I struggled with the demands of the game.

In retrospect, my final match in an All Black jersey being against Wales had a strange symmetry to it. Wales had loomed large in my father's career, and now it was playing against them at their temporary home at Wembley that I was to have my swansong. Of course, at the time I didn't realise or accept that fully. After I came off in that match, I still worked hard to get the knee right for the Ireland match that was up next. Talking to my good mate Zinzan Brooke gave me what turned out to be false hope – Zinny told me I was playing well, that no one would ever notice, and that I should crack on and play. There was also a degree of interest in the press too – I was approaching one hundred caps, and while personally I genuinely took little notice, rugby pundits enjoyed the 'Will he, won't he?' story that broke when my knee flared up again.

I had been very clear with the then-coach of the All Blacks – a good friend of mine, John Hart – and vice versa, he had been very straightforward with me. We had agreed that we would be straight with each other regarding my position in the team. I knew that he wouldn't just drop me, but rather he would talk to me first and allow me to make my own decision. I appreciated that. I had made a commitment to myself that I would finish at the top of my game and not let myself slide into being a poorer, older version, running on empty and trundling round the pitch remembering the good times. For me, the measure of that was simple – I would not get dropped from the All Blacks. I would play on until either I or Harty thought that the end was in sight. At that point, I would make the decision to stop.

I talked honestly to Harty about my knee.

In the middle of the week running up to the Ireland game, I told him that it was time to select another hooker.

I wasn't going to make it – at least not to the standard that I wanted to play to and the standard that the All Black jersey demanded. Painful, tough moments, and while I had no hesitation in having the conversation, I struggled with actually saying the words. I had

Aside from my knee, I was still as strong as a bull . . . to acknowledge therefore that a key part of my body had given out on me and that I could no longer lead from the front was to acknowledge that many things – in fact, *everything* – was about to change.

fought tooth and claw to gain and retain my New Zealand Number 2 jersey. Aside from my knee, I was still as strong as a bull. My mind was sharp, my appetite undiminished. I felt that I still had a good deal to offer the team from a leadership point of view. To acknowledge therefore that a key part of my body had given out on me and that I could no longer lead from the front was to acknowledge that many things – in fact, *everything* – was about to change.

Harty allowed me to tell the squad. I know that there would have been one guy bouncing with happiness inside (and bloody right too, so he should have been, I wouldn't expect or want anything else from the new All Black hooker!), but there was also an element of disbelief. I had been around a long time and I hadn't shared the extent of the injury with many of the guys, so I suppose the expectation was that I would just shake it off and all would be well. I don't mind telling you that I was upset, and that I had a tear in my eye when I told the lads. I knew that once you give your jersey away, it can be bloody hard to get it back again.

I prepared for the Ireland game pretty much as usual, right down to the phone call home that had become a ritual over the years. The folks back in New Zealand were of course concerned for me, but I played it down. I watched the game and supported the boys and worked hard to project a philosophical but optimistic tone when the press came calling.

Inside though it was a different story. If I look back on that time now I can see that the biggest issue for me was the element of the unknown. I was party to the usual feelings when a big change like this appears to be taking place in someone's life – there was a little bit of anger about it happening. I was probably in denial about the finality of it all, and I certainly had moments when I had fears about what the future would ultimately hold for me; but the really difficult aspect for me to handle was no longer being clear on what I controlled any more. It was that lack of certainty (or perhaps more accurately the removal of all the certainty in my life) that wobbled me most. For almost as long as I could remember, I had been Sean Fitzpatrick the All Black, or Sean Fitzpatrick the All Black captain. My rugby had pretty much defined me . . . and now that definition had been removed. I had been in a very structured rugby set-up right from my earliest days at the local club and all the way through school. I'd worked my way through the provincial and national representative sides until I had become an All Black, and then I had stayed in the national side for about a decade, half of that time as captain. The conversation I had just had with Harty put an end to that part of my life. My All Black career was now behind me and I had some adjusting to do.

AN IDEA TO TRY: ANTICIPATE CHANGE, MANAGE CHANGE, AND ENJOY IT

Whatever the change is that you find yourself having to deal with, you have to try to keep your focus on working it cleverly and with focus. Change will keep happening and it will remain relentless. To really drive change, rather than have it happen to you, you have to *fail fast, learn fast, fix fast.* By that I mean that it won't be a smooth, beautifully crafted process of change to get from where you are to where you need to be. There are likely to be challenges, unexpected problems, and as yet unthought-of possibilities that will present themselves to you along the way – so be attentive to them. When you drop the ball, make sure you don't sit there beating yourself up about it. Get up, move on. Fix it and maintain momentum.

You also have to work out what you can't affect, and park it. Let it go, leave it aside. What is left is the stuff you can work on, work with and work out. Focus on that first, and make a start. There is no point in rumbling along worrying about dark imaginings or factors that are out of your control. Control the controllables.

But first of all I had to say goodbye. I embarked on a crazy few months after I announced my retirement from rugby football where I was awarded the New Zealand Order of Merit (a proud moment), was made guest of honour at a number of farewell dinners, and stood in stadiums while people clapped and cheered and said thank you. It was a genuinely touching and wonderful time, which really did help me to work through any frustration and sadness that I still had at finishing my playing career. It was a pleasure to be feted! I took a deep and genuine satisfaction out of the fact that people treated me so kindly, said so many nice things to me, and thanked me for my contribution to All Black rugby, and I was allowed to move on from being pissed off to being hugely grateful that I had enjoyed the career I'd had.

One of the questions that I do keep getting asked is whether or not I miss the game at all. My answer is that I don't. Not really. I do have the occasional twinge when a big game comes along, but for the most

I certainly had moments when I had fears about what the future would ultimately hold for me; but the really difficult aspect for me to handle was no longer being clear on what I controlled any more.

part I am contented to have hung up my boots. Interestingly I think that having two girls has really helped me to put a little bit of distance between the game and me. If I had had a boy, of course he would have played – and with a huge amount of expectation on his shoulders too, poor fella – and I suspect that I would be right in the middle of the whole scene again. But the life of an international rugby player is a hard one. There are long tours and a lot of time away from home and your loved ones. The physical demands are high, and the training regime can be brutal. I think that, all in all, I ended up getting out of the game at a good time for me in terms of age and experience, and although hugely and passionately grateful to the sport, I also confess to a small amount of relief at not having to keep going.

That individual circumstance of finally reaching the end of a period of high performance and beginning to dip – that I sensed I was on the cusp of when my knee went before the Ireland game – also happens to whole teams. As I mentioned in Chapter 5, one of the interesting features about an international squad, even a consistently excellent side like the All Blacks, is that it goes in phases. For a while, there are a number of changes, people come and go and the coach is looking to build a cohesive core of players but still moving people around to find the combinations. In the ideal world, that turns into a period of continuity, where players begin to get settled in their position, the squad and the team begins to function effectively and it feels good. The third phase is where it over-cooks – players get too relaxed or complacent or just too plain old, and the performance starts to dip. At that point the coach (at least the good coaches!) will recognise the need to move players on and out, and the process of 'rebuilding' the team starts again. In some cases, a team may need to be rebuilt after losing a single player. It is time to change.

This idea of a cycle is certainly not a new one – it is well recognised and any of you who follow a sports team will be familiar with the concept, but it is interesting to draw the same parallel with work and family teams. Okay, I accept that it is difficult to move team members out of your family team – unless you embark on some pretty drastic action you have the same players with you all the way though your life – but nonetheless, it is good to recognise that the work team and the family team around you are also fluid, dynamic entities, and not solid immovable units of constancy. They will go through cycles of change too, and recognising when they need refreshing, rebuilding, remotivating or re-energising is important.

One of the key skills in life, I think, is recognising when it is time for a change. Sometimes that is hard – situations creep up on you, or the sands shift beneath your feet while you're looking the other way, or concentrating on the task in hand. Have you heard about the frog in water? I don't know if it is true or not (and have no overwhelming urge to check it out) but it goes that if you put a frog into boiling water, it will hop out, whereas if you put it in cold water and then heat the water up to boiling point, the frog will sit there, and eventually die. I think it is a really interesting analogy to life. When we are put into a stressful or obviously life-changing situation, we react . . . but if the need for change develops over years, and creeps up on us, how many of us are able to spot that and react . . . and how many of us just continue to sit there, doing the same thing as before?

AN IDEA TO TRY: FAILURE CAN DRIVE CHANGE

Remember to let failure stoke the fire. Whenever I was in a losing All Black dressing room, I drank it in. I really did. I didn't want to just get changed and go to the bar to drown my sorrows; well, honestly speaking, perhaps I did, but I also needed to maximise my experience so that I could recall the smells, the sounds, the feeling of defeat. I put it all in my head and I pulled it out again to remind me just how bad it felt. I used it to motivate myself never to have to feel or experience it again. I used it as an agent for change. And I still do. I still use it as a spur to look at the options, the alternatives and to motivate me to put the changes in motion. It doesn't matter that the situations and challenges that I face these days when I am dealing with change are not always specifically rugby related. The feeling of failure is the same, and I will change whatever I need to change in order that I don't have to feel it again.

Of course a lot of this is to do with environment. If change is a once-in-a-lifetime process, it will inevitably be difficult but if on the other hand it is a normal part of your everyday life, it becomes a whole lot easier to manage. Formula One as a sport, and Ross Brawn in particular, is worth looking at when seeing how to handle and manage change. Formula One is probably one of the most dynamic and fast-moving competitions in the world. Every year there seem to be new regulations and limitations; teams develop technologies to give their drivers a millisecond advantage, and the whole concept of getting the most out of a car on a particular day often involves managing a huge amount of change, sometimes in a very short space of time and under severe pressure. That Ross Brawn could turn a situation where the team he worked for was going to pull out of F1 into a situation where he created and led a team that won the World Championship in its first year of existence is absolute testimony to the man. There will be books written about how he did it of course – and I look forward to reading them! – but in that single year, as Brawn F1 re-wrote the history books (before the team became part of the Mercedes machine), three things absolutely shone out for me. The first is that the man is clearly a perfectionist. Excellence is the minimum requirement for Brawn, and that pays dividends in his chosen sport. There are no 'holy cows' and no exceptions, he will scrutinise and look to make anything better, more competitive. He is being the best that he can be. The second thing about him is linked to this excellence. He has an absolute clarity of outcome – he is a man who is very clear on what he and his team are aiming to do. He fixes himself on an outcome and then bends his will and the will of others working around him. The third, and perhaps the most interesting with regard to this chapter is that Ross Brawn seems to embrace change. He, and the organisation he quickly built around him at Brawn F1 encouraged it, fed off it, and thrived on it. They seemed geared completely towards coping with – and taking maximum advantage of – changes in track position, regulations, driver performance, weather. Whatever the variable, Brawn and his team seemed to have both the systems and methods to handle the situation, but more than that the attitude and unshakable belief that they could manage the change to best effect, and to their own advantage. Throughout

I had been Sean Fitzpatrick the
All Black, or Sean Fitzpatrick the
All Black captain. My rugby had
pretty much defined me . . . and
now that definition had been
removed.

that team's hugely successful season in Formula One, time and time again Ross Brawn and his team were a perfect example of how to take change and, instead of passively reacting to it, to really drive it. (I know, a dreadful pun, but I hope you take the point . . .). It was compelling to watch.

Partway through my career as an All Black, the New Zealand Rugby Union dared to change a facet of Kiwi rugby culture that had been perceived by many as utterly unchangeable. The All Black rugby kit was all black, except for the silver fern on the breast, the white collar on the jersey, and the two white bands around the top of the socks. Remember those socks? The coveted, prized All Black socks that I would wear out running when I thought no one would see me just because of how it felt to have them on? Now this may sound absurd to those of you who aren't Kiwis, but the All Black identity was defined by the two white bands on the socks and there was huge opposition and unhappiness across New Zealand when it was announced that there was a prospect of changing them. The difficulty was that Adidas, the newly signed official kit makers, had a logo that was all about three stripes and it was inevitable that the change was going to happen. I understood the reservations completely too. The Originals had two stripes on their socks and a hundred years' worth of All Black rugby was played with two stripes. Why on earth should we change for commercial reasons, particularly as the change was being imposed by an overseas sports brand?

Adidas was taking on the very identity of New Zealanders when they made the change, and they did it superbly. They had clearly done their homework and they understood the depth of feeling that existed, so they ran a national TV ad that engaged people in the change and allayed their concerns. The ad was only 30 or so seconds long, and it simply showed a rugby changing room. In it, the opening shot was of the oldest living captain C.K. Saxton (1945–46) in his original All Black jersey. In a close-up shot, he pulls another jersey down over his head and when the head came through and the camera pans back a bit, you can see that it is the next captain of the All Blacks in the jersey that he wore. With simple, stirring music playing underneath, the process continued until it got to Taine Randell, the captain after me and the incumbent when the ad was run. When I pulled the jersey down over my head, Randell pops out and the jersey he has got on has the Adidas logo on the right breast across from the Silver Fern. The camera snaps right back – but only for about a millisecond – to show the three stripes on the socks and then a big final line of text fills the screen that says, 'The legacy is more intimidating than any opposition.' It was brilliant. It engaged people emotionally, and it showed that the overseas sports company understood what it was to be an All Black and how important the All Blacks are to New Zealand. In effect, Adidas made a promise to the New Zealand people – their ad showed a commitment to retaining the soul of the All Black brand and consequently people relaxed a wee bit. The two stripes became three, the All Blacks kept winning, and Adidas remains kit sponsor to this day. My dad never relaxed about it though, to be fair!

I mention this advert here because it highlights that you can sell in even difficult changes if you engage with people, talk to them and recognise their map of the world and how they see things. If you are straightforward enough, or perhaps brave enough to tackle the issues that arise out of a change with honesty and directness, you can make things happen.

When I look back on the changes that I have been a part of –

either initiating them or being on the receiving end of them – it becomes clear to me that managing change isn't actually about the decision to change itself. That is the easy part. Managing change, or driving change, is all about how you handle the consequences and the impact of the decision that you've made and how you make that handling positively intentioned. People generally wobble when change is taking place. Some wobble more, some less (and a very few not at all, but only a few) depending on how motivated they are by the change, and whether they stand to gain or lose from it personally. Even their general attitude to life will have a bearing on how an individual handles change. You drive change by ensuring that when the wobbling is happening, you are there. You must provide a steadying, encouraging hand and if you can point the way to a clear and positive outcome, people will, in time, gain in confidence and belief. In times of change, you have to keep faith with your plan. You have to stick to your guns, trust your judgement in terms of direction, and soldier on. Be adaptable certainly (and if it really is a dreadful idea then I hope you have the sense to see it!) but once you've struck out from the shore, keep bloody swimming. People do like things to stay the same, so when change is happening it can become a negative process, unless they 'own' the change – by which I mean that they feel engaged in the process and enjoy a sense of responsibility for making it happen, that they feel like they've got a stake in it and that it is the right course of action. Then, the process can be much more powerful and longer-lasting.

Fixing on a positive outcome – even using fear as a key motivating factor to make it real and immediate – is the way to get your head right so that your performance follows.

AN IDEA TO TRY: WHAT WOULD YOU DO IF . . .?

Here is a simple question to ask yourself when you are in a period of change and you find it daunting or scary. What would you do if you weren't afraid? Being excited about what could be is a great place to get to, and though we seem to be coached and directed in life to follow the more conservative, reactive, sensible path, sometimes that just isn't enough, and taking a fear-free decision is the brave – and the right – thing to do. So what would you do if you weren't afraid?

'Moving towards' is a much more powerful direction than 'moving away from' and when everything around you is changing, it is tempting to react to the change, rather than to look at where the change can take you. It's a tough nut to crack but one of the lessons I have learnt that has been invaluable to me in my post-rugby life has been this idea about moving towards something – having specific targets and outcomes – rather than getting stuck in the 'I don't want to do this or that' mindset. That's a trap.

AN IDEA TO TRY: A COUPLE MORE IDEAS

Firstly, the most important aspect about change is knowing what not to change. To do one, three or 30 new things, you will probably have to stop doing a similar number of things. So what are they? What are you going to stop doing so that you can 'start' doing something else? To help you structure your thoughts, use these four headings. What are you going to:

a) Create

b) Increase

c) Reduce

d) Eliminate

Secondly, acting 'as if' is a useful tool when you are handling change. Act 'as if' the change has already happened. Get to grips with what it feels like, start wearing the clothes, walking the walk. It makes it more real, more immediate, more likely. More tangible.

One thing I have noticed in the business world is that motivation is much more often discussed when there is a problem or an issue with it in the business. Generally when the issue of team or business motivation is on the agenda, it is because there isn't any! Of course you and I can both name a dozen examples of places where this isn't the case, but perhaps these notable exceptions prove the rule. Too many businesses and business leaders only pay attention to this vitally important ingredient after it has become a problem, whereas I think in sport it is recognised much earlier as a crucial component to success.

Motivation in a time of change is all about making people feel good. Giving people decisions to make, responsibility, belief and authority has a huge positive impact on people. Thinking about how you can make people feel good about the decisions that you have to make is important. You don't *have* to think about it and spend the time to work out how to present it positively, but if you can and do it does pay you back. When it comes to coaching, one thing I found out pretty early on after I stopped playing is that I don't really like coaching rugby players in a technical sense. I'm certainly not a technician, the sort of coach who can make you a better scrummager or line-out thrower by providing a detailed breakdown of lines of pressure or trajectories. And if I got my hands on the backs I could probably do untold damage to their game. Instead, I much prefer to work – and think I add more value this way – with the mental side of playing. Mentally I think I can help players to hone and apply their skills with the right mental attitude. You can change that; fix it, improve it and achieve better results because of that. Harbouring a positive mental attitude sounds a bit tired and clichéd these days, but that is because it is true, and has always been true. Fixing on a positive outcome – even using fear as a key motivating factor to make it real and immediate – is the way to get your head right so that your performance follows.

One way of thinking that really helped me in handling change was having a very clear view on what those things are that are most important to me. My wife and my family have provided me with stability and balance, and that has helped me keep a degree of equilibrium even when a lot of other parts of my life have been up in the air. Even as captain, having Bronnie, and later the kids, was a vital anchor for me, keeping me rooted and grounded. By having that constant there, other change was easier to manage, and I think that there is a useful idea in there. Change happens, but not allowing it to happen on too many fronts at the same time is important – you need to have a degree of stability and continuity somewhere in your life. There may be times and situations where radical, across-the-board changes are the right answer. But remember too that we human beings are sensitive machines sometimes. To put us under too much pressure from too many directions can have unintended negative consequences. I have certainly known and been close to people that have really struggled with change and with all the demands that are either being placed on them, or sometimes that they are placing on themselves. With too many things going on at the same time, it is easy to get out of kilter, confused, or stressed, and not do anything properly. Having that continuity and stability of areas in your life that are *not* changing means that you can channel your focus and enjoy the process of change where it is happening, rather than feeling like you are fighting it or drowning in it. I have found myself more often than not excited about the possibilities that lie before me and I believe that in part this is due to having my anchor of family firmly in place.

A FINAL THOUGHT ON DRIVING CHANGE

As the weeks and months began to pass, I started getting used to life as an ex-All Black. I wanted to look forward not back, and although I was clear that rugby was going to remain central to my life, I had decided that coaching wasn't for me. Bronnie and I talked long and hard about what I should do and where I should be heading, and increasingly it seemed to us that we had a clear choice in front of us. One option was to settle down in New Zealand. I could carve out a nice living speaking at dinners, working with New Zealand companies, and writing articles and commentating. Or we could

Managing change, or driving change, is all about how you handle the consequences and the impact of the decision that you've made and how you make that handling positively intentioned.

embark on an adventure. We could move to the other side of the world, and take our chances in trying to make a go of developing a career as a business consultant and speaker where there were more companies and more opportunities, but where perhaps I was less well known. We made our choice. We packed up, and shipped out to London.

NINE

FRONTING UP

IF I LOOK AT THE DIFFERENT phases of my life, I think that in one way or another I have always been fighting to keep my head above the water line. Almost literally on occasion . . . when I was eight or nine my older brother and his mates decided to torment me with an improvised water torture. They staked me out like a starfish on the front lawn and dripped (poured!) water from a hosepipe onto my head. My sister got in on the act too when she walked past, by pulling my pants down. There I was, de-bagged, immobile, soaking wet, and wailing for my mum . . . deeply traumatic stuff! And I remember my mum coming out to the front step, taking in the whole scene, and simply saying, 'Mark, let Sean go!' before turning back into the house. It is funny now when I look back on it, but I do wonder whether being the youngest with rowdy older kids around taught me the importance of resilience and how to take tough shots. I always wanted to play with the big kids and despite getting pushed up against the back window in the car, getting kicked and punched in the good-natured way that older kids do to remind you who's the boss, I kept going back for more. I loved it. We had a wonderful home life. It wasn't sunshine and skittles all the time and we had to watch the pennies and make do with what we had (I know, I know, all that stuff that people always say when they get a bit older . . . but it is *true*!) but it was a great way to grow up and I believe that I benefited from picking up both a work ethic and a fighting ethic that has been great for me. I strongly suspect that I have my family – and in particular Mark and his mates – to thank for developing my ability to fight my corner, to front up to people, to challenges.

Fronting up to a new life was what I did when we moved to England. Having such a strong connection with my family meant that moving to the UK was a real challenge. We came to England in 2003, some six years after my last game in an All Black jersey and it was a major change in our lives. We had to sort out all the logistics of getting a home. We started out in rented accommodation. We had all the usual house-moving stuff to contend with, and on top of that we were finding schools, opening bank accounts, working out the peculiarities of British bureaucracy . . . lots to keep us busy besides the small matter of making a living! In fact in the long run it has turned out to have been a great move for myself and for the family, but in the first few months it was hard. Not least because I did (and still do) miss New Zealand a wee bit. I do get back home often enough that I still feel connected, but I spent so much of my life there and my friends and ties – particularly my rugby ties – are so strong there that not being around took some getting used to.

BACKGROUND

Funnily enough, having left New Zealand, one of the rugby ties that I perhaps miss the most comes to mind every time I see a photograph that I have, that still brings a smile to my face today – a group shot of the Monday night touch rugby boys. Happy days. When I lived back in New Zealand, I was part of a mixed bunch of like-minded blokes who got together every Monday for a run-out. We'd meet at 4.30 Monday afternoon and play touch rugby (a non-contact version of the game) for an hour or two. With no referee, the decision-making was highly democratic! We would occasionally re-enact New Zealand vs South Africa games (the All Blacks would win of course), I would display some silky champagne-rugby skills (it's my book and I shall write it up as I remember it), and we'd play hard and have some great chat. Touch rugby is a sociable game, and I remember those evenings with much fondness. That photograph reminds me of the importance of the team, of team spirit, of banter and belonging. It was never just about keeping fit. It was much more to do with staying connected to those things that have always been important in my life – standing alongside a group of mates, beating the opposition. The closeness and camaraderie, the belonging and enjoyment that makes being a part of a team a great place to be.

Every human being (apart from one or two notable exceptions that I have met along the way who shall remain nameless) enjoys being part

Fronting up is an enjoyable process. It isn't some dour noble cause for which you should be martyred, or something that gives no return, no payback. It is a challenge, and the experience of rising to it is there to be enjoyed.

of something bigger than themselves. We enjoy committing to a larger cause, we thrive on shared journeys, on communal achievement, and we often become the best that we can be when we work with and for others. It has been a deep and genuine joy to me that I had the time and the experiences that I had, both at the Monday night touch rugby, and within the All Black set-up – where matches were ferocious rather than fun, and where it was deadly serious. There is something elemental, fundamental about growling at an opponent, squaring up and looking him in the eye and knowing that as soon as the whistle goes you are going to knock lumps out of him. It is war and I am convinced that it is not dissimilar to how men feel, act and react in real battles, where the stakes are highest: your life or the life of the other guy. There is a basic drive, a need to dominate, a need to win that becomes apparent within rugby that I think strikes a chord at a much deeper level than just that of a game. It is part of rugby's appeal and it is why it appeals to so many. There is no other sport in the world, in my opinion, that is purer or more exposing. It strips away the bullshit and the posturing and you are left with two sides going to war. Tactics play a part, and like all good victories, generals can influence the outcome. But in the final analysis, it is the players on the pitch, the warriors standing toe-to-toe and trading blows that define the outcome. You are defined by your actions in the heat of battle, not in how you look or sound in the run-up to the match, not at the press conference afterwards, or at the celebrity-laden evening later on, but on the pitch. When you either front up or you don't.

I am sure that all of us can recall people we went to school with, or that we have met along life's way, whose talent was high but whose application, or appreciation of the hard work involved, or lack of desire to win meant that they did not make the most out of their talent. There are some people I have played with, even at international standard, that appeared to have been quite happy going through life at a cruise. As an All Black, one or two boys contented themselves with just being a good All Black when they could have been great. I hope that doesn't sound churlish – I know there are many players who have worked immensely hard and never been given the opportunity of playing at that level, but my point is that whatever level you play at, you come across guys who are tryers and guys who coast along. I could never be like that, and I got bloody annoyed with anyone who was. I still do.

I don't understand it either, because fronting up – and that is what we are talking about – is an enjoyable process. It isn't some dour noble cause for which you should be martyred, or something that gives no return, no payback. It is a challenge, and the experience of rising to it is there to be enjoyed. You have to be prepared for the fight of course, but the inner comfort and strength that you can draw from having made the clear decision that you are going to face whatever is coming is in itself energising. The knowledge that you will face whatever challenge lies ahead, and that you will make the best of it, is in my opinion a real gift to yourself, if you are able to give it. It is an attitude of mind that breeds fortitude, resilience and optimism. It is worth pursuing.

Fronting up also means not hiding behind the measurable. What do I mean by that? There is a growing reliance on analysis, numbers, statistics and percentages in the modern world – in sport, in government, in business, in life. It is easy, comforting, expected almost to ensure that decisions are based on these numbers – that the competitive environment or situation is analysed and systemised, and that the individual decision-maker has to interpret the numbers in order to make the right decision. True, but also false. True because the facts and figures can inform you and you'd be a fool to ignore them – but centring your entire approach in this way is to deny the sorcery and brilliance that can exist through insight, through gut feel, and through doing the unexpected. Within sport, it is the age-old conundrum of getting players to play within a system, to learn their part in the process and to discourage them from departing from the plan, versus the school of thought that says a player should be given the authority and responsibility to play what they see, to make decisions, to be creative.

It might also be that the numbers or the analysis or reason all suggest that it would be folly to even start. The numbers might be stacked against you, but fronting up means having a go, and trying to make a difference, however insignificant or futile it may appear. I heard this story that I think illustrates the point beautifully – if you have heard it told better, my apologies, but as I recall it goes like this: a guy was driving down the coast road in Mexico, and running alongside the road was a beach, miles long. On the beach were hundreds of thousands of starfish that had been washed up in the high tide and that were now dead or dying in the hot sun. As the guy drove along, he saw, way off in the distance, a single kid down by the water's edge. As he got closer, he realised that the kid was picking up starfish and throwing them into the sea. The guy stopped the car, wandered down the beach and asked the boy what he was doing. 'I'm saving the starfish,' the boy replied. The guy laughed. 'Saving the starfish? This beach must have millions of starfish on it – what you're doing will make absolutely no difference.' The boy smiled, and as he picked up another starfish and threw it back into the sea he said to the man, 'Well, I just made a difference to that one.'

You decide on the difference you make, both to starfish, other people, and to yourself. You have to take responsibility for your own happiness and not just let yourself be led or steered or influenced by others. You own your life, no one else does, and whatever hand has been dealt to you, you have to try to play it as best you can. You can choose your attitude. If you want to be pissed off, you can be pissed off. If you want to be the best that you can be, then you can be that too. You decide.

Fronting up becomes more important precisely as it becomes harder. The points at which other people would give up, or take an easy option, those are exactly the moments when fronting up differentiates you from everyone else. That is what makes you successful. Whatever the pressure, not accepting the status quo if you don't believe in it is absolutely the right thing to do. Sometimes you have to take a principled decision and stick with it, even if the outcome isn't palatable or if you're not going to be popular as a result of it. Sometimes you have to stand your ground. Front up.

When Kevin Roberts met us All Blacks for the first time, he wasn't a happy bunny. He was CEO of Lion Nathan and their best-selling beer Steinlager was the number one sponsor of All Black rugby. He was annoyed that as a squad we spent very little time with the sponsor's guests, we kept ourselves to ourselves at dinners, and we drank whatever brand of beer we felt like. He fronted up and gave us a collective dressing down. It probably wasn't the smartest thing to do from a diplomatic perspective, and I suspect that it broke all the rules about how to get the most out of the team you're responsible for developing an ongoing relationship with, but he fronted up, said what was on his mind, and risked pissing off the entire squad in order to make what he thought was an important point.

Rugby is not about being on the back foot, reacting and trying to minimise damage. It is not about avoiding confrontation or shying away from adversity. It is about creation, fierce and focused. It is about meeting challenge head-on, about winning.

As it happened, a couple of us repaid the compliment of fronting up, and we unloaded a few home truths of our own. We weren't motivated or engaged with the whole sponsorship thing, and why would we be? We were basically treated like slabs of meat – wheeled in and wheeled out again for event after event, and yet we saw nothing material in return come back to the team. We felt our training equipment needed upgrading, our Number Ones (our official suits) were poor, we travelled steerage class at the back of the plane, and all in all we felt like we were at the very end of a very long line, and that not much was actually getting back to us. As it transpired, Kevin was a fixer. He got us sorted, and in return we sorted Kevin out – so by fronting up to the issues, we all benefited.

As a leader, fronting up has external implications – because how you come across is important. It's not all just about how you come to terms with change or challenges yourself; there are others to consider and their view on the world needs to be thought about. I have heard a number of really useful and insightful quotes about leadership in my time, and a couple of them I think relate specifically to this notion of fronting up. One that I am particularly fond of is that a good leader will take people where they want to go, whereas a great leader will take them not necessarily where they want to go, but where they need to be. In that phrase is an implied need to front up – to not take the easy path, but to take the right one. That sometimes means having to front up with the team, which is not always a comfortable place to be, and it can be a lonely business.

AN IDEA TO TRY: BEING AUTHENTIC

Authenticity is vitally important. If you are trying to pretend, to act your way to success, you're doomed. People will find you out. So make sure that you are genuine and authentic in everything that you do. If you want to be the best people manager in the company, then don't go home, grump around the place, shout at the kids and fight with your wife or husband. There is no work/life balance in my book, only work/life integration, and whether you are talking to a small kid, a *Big Issue* seller or a global CEO, you should be genuine, authentic. And however difficult, intense or personal it might get when you are fronting up, look for the positive outcome. Aim to express yourself with comfort and with confidence. Don't hesitate or question yourself. Step up and put your view across. Do so with a positive intention, and with a positive outcome in mind.

Another great quote that makes me smile is the one that says it is hard to lead a cavalry charge if you think that you look funny on a horse. You have to front up to the fact that you are the leader. Those inner doubts can hinder you; a lack of certainty is unhelpful. Do you remember the Andy Dalton meeting where I thought I wasn't up to the job when I was first made captain of the All Blacks? As I found out then, you have to commit fully to your enterprise. It is only by jumping in with heart and soul that you give yourself the opportunity to give it your best shot, to be the best that you can be. There is no value in holding back, no merit in keeping an emergency exit half-open or worrying about whether the parachute will open. You have to jump, and commit.

As I mentioned before, periodically these days people ask me about my 'leadership style'. I try to make my approach to answering these questions much like how I played – practical and direct. I don't think that I was a great speech-maker before matches. I led by example. I think that it was an approach that serves well – even up here in England! Elsewhere, a perfect example of fronting up not needing to be about speeches and theory, but about action and physical leadership comes from the not-so-recent Rugby World Cup-winning England side. Martin Johnson was their captain. He was always going to be a good player, courtesy of his All Black training in New Zealand (in fact I believe his first ever international match as a junior was for the All Blacks) but as captain for England he didn't do the big speeches or strategic tactical insights. He simply led by example and put himself about with such ferocity that he bred similar desires in those around him. He was a man who fronted up on the pitch. Jason Leonard (a stalwart of the England team for years – and a tough boy) recently said of Martin Johnson that he'd walk over broken glass for him. He also said that if Martin asked him to run through a brick wall he'd do it, although he would know that 'Johnners' would have already got there first and punched the hole in the wall for him to go through. That really resonated with me – leadership is about showing what you want by how you act, by fronting up. Banging into walls and creating the holes for your people to follow is a pretty good way of doing that.

A little closer to home is Richie McCaw, the current All Black captain as I write this. He plays the most games, he makes the most hits, and he is consistently one of the best players on the paddock. He is ferocious, he puts his body on the line time and time again, and he is the first name on the team sheet when the coach picks his side. Richie McCaw is loved by his players and feared by his opponents. I for one would have loved to have had him in my team because he is the perfect player to show you that rugby in general, but All Black rugby in particular, is not about being on the back foot, reacting and trying to minimise damage. It is not about avoiding confrontation or shying away from adversity. It is about creation, fierce and focused. It is about meeting challenge head-on, about winning. Runner-up is not acceptable; second-best is not an option. In any 80 minutes you care to watch you can see those messages being sent out by McCaw. Everything about the way he plays suggests to the other team: our approach is based on courage and conviction, we have a solid game plan, and it is executed with ferocity and belief – you'd better watch out. Great stuff.

But fronting up is not only all about barrelling into the ugly mutt on the other team and making his afternoon miserable by getting on his case from the first second – although that certainly has its attractions – but it is also (and perhaps even more importantly) an internal perspective too. It means being yourself. It means coming to terms with yourself – your shortcomings and your strengths, the bits you like and the elements you dislike. It means knowing what you are good at and what you are not good at. And it means following your hunches and your gut feel. Fronting up is all about having an attitude of facing whatever is put in front of you, but it is not just about aggression and combative confrontation. It is also about pushing yourself, fronting up to your own inner demons and doubts. Facing your own fears and weaknesses is, for me, perhaps the purest form of fronting up. Being strong enough to look with objectivity and dispassion at your own failings and shortcomings, to chart a course

You own your life, no one
else does, and whatever
hand has been dealt to you,
you have to try to play it as
best you can.

through them, and to come out the other side, is a cool thing to be able to do. It puts you in the enviable position of knowing yourself.

A word of caution though: don't unnecessarily expose your failings, weaknesses or shortcomings; wherever possible, play to your strengths. The glorious defeat never sat well with me as either a Kiwi or an All Black, and to win ugly is my choice every time, no contest, but while fronting up is easy on the rugby pitch, it doesn't mean being dumb with regard to life in general! I hope that you remain smart enough to know when to get into a confrontation and when to avoid it. In life, perhaps more so than in rugby, it is true that a good retreat is better than a bad stand. Sometimes ducking the issue is the smart thing to do, the right thing to do. The challenge lies in being continuously honest with yourself about why you have ducked or avoided a particular situation. If it is the best option, fine. If it is the easy option . . . not fine.

If you are going to be the best that you can be, you are going to have to front up, and get it sorted. There is always a time when the need to talk, to analyse, to consider, to weigh up, to defer, is past. There is always a time when you have to front up. Rugby is simply a game to shift a ball over a line. It is all about the ball. Too much analysis and complication can lead to teams taking their eye off that simple truth; layering on too much and being too clever by half means they forget the simple truth of what they're trying to do. In the best teams, the best players know that when the whistle blows for the start of the match you have to set your shoulder to the wheel. You have to hump the bloody ball over the line. It is all about the outcome, not the process, and whatever it takes, it has to be done. You have to work hard, make sacrifices, strain and fight. You simply have to get it done.

AN IDEA TO TRY: FRONTING UP SOMETIMES MEANS CONFRONTATION

Fronting up means getting into the odd dogfight. That's fine. Remember the saying – 'It's not the size of the dog in the fight, it's the size of the fight in the dog.' If you are going to front up, then front up. It really is no more complicated than that. If you have to fight your corner then do so. If you have to deliver difficult news, that is part of the process. If you find the world against you and you know you're right, then keep going. A positive intention, and the acceptance of the possibility of having to fight are a liberating combination. Knowing what you want, and being prepared to fight for it puts you at the front of the pack.

And you might as well start now. Nothing is worth more than this day. Living for today rather than living on the past or dreaming about tomorrow is all a part of fronting up effectively. Every game could be your last. I suppose I was lucky in that I knew about and fought against my career-ending injury – but for many, it comes out of the blue. Sudden and juddering, your life changes fundamentally when you can no longer play the sport that you have enjoyed since way back when. I suspect that the same is true of life. The Robin Williams film *Dead Poets Society* was a cracking movie, and it gave rise to the popularisation of the phrase '*carpe diem*' – seize the day. It may have become popular just because it was a bloody good film, but I don't think so. I think that became a phrase that people tuned

Fronting up becomes more important precisely as it becomes harder . . . that is what makes you successful.

into and picked up because it taps into the deep and honest fear that we all know but that we keep to the back of our minds. The certainty of our own mortality is not a great subject to dwell on for any great length of time, but the message that you have to seize the day today certainly is.

And that relies on character. In my experience, character beats intellect every single time. Whatever skills or abilities or attributes you possess, whatever gifts have been given to you, without character they are weakened and diluted. Character forges those gifts, talents and attributes. How you manage them, use them, appreciate them and harness them will in my opinion dictate the degree to which you will succeed in your chosen field.

A FINAL THOUGHT ON FRONTING UP

You have to decide whether to take the easy option or take the tough, sometimes painful road. My choice? Front up. Every time. For better or for worse, both on and off the pitch, I am quite happy to say: This is me, and this is who I am. This is what I stand for, and this is my life. It's my ball, and it's my game. If you want to beat me, or better me, then give it a go, but know that from the moment it starts until the moment it is over, I will not lie down, I will not step backwards, I will not give you an inch. You had better be at your *very* best, because if you're not, if you have any doubts at all, they'll be laid bare. I will front up.

So that is the message to you, too. There are always a million and one reasons that you can find for not doing something, or for continuing to do something that isn't allowing you to become the best that you can be. It's too hard. It's too easy. It's lonely, or it's too much of a risk . . . the list goes on and on.

So you have a simple choice. You have to decide. Do you stand up or step aside?

To be the best that you can be, front up.

INDEX

ABOUT THE CO-AUTHOR

Andy FitzGerald is the Human Resources Director for Alfred Dunhill Ltd, an English men's luxury brand within the Richemont Group. A lifelong rugby enthusiast, writer on sport and business, and junior rugby coach at Chipstead RFC, Andy lives in Epsom, Surrey, together with his wife Carrie and their four children: Ciara, Archie, Niamh and Liam . . . all of whom already possess a more effective sidestep than he ever had.